I'm STILL STANDING

Published by
The Bible Reading Fellowship
First Floor, Elsfield Hall
15–17 Elsfield Way, Oxford OX2 8FG
Website: www.brf.org.uk

ISBN 1 84101 349 8
First published 2005
10 9 8 7 6 5 4 3 2 1 0
All rights reserved

Acknowledgments
Unless otherwise indicated, scripture quotations are taken from the Holy
Bible, New Living Translation, copyright 1996. Used by permission of
Tyndale House Publishers, Inc., Wheaton, Illinois 60189. All rights reserved.

Scripture quotations taken from the Holy Bible, New International Version,
copyright © 1973, 1978, 1984 by International Bible Society, are used by
permission of Hodder & Stoughton Limited. All rights reserved. 'NIV' is a
registered trademark of International Bible Society. UK trademark number
1448790.

Scriptures quoted from the Good News Bible published by The Bible
Societies/HarperCollins Publishers Ltd, UK © American Bible Society 1966,
1971, 1976, 1992, are used with permission.

Scripture quotations from the Contemporary English Version © American
Bible Society 1991, 1992, 1995. Used by permission/Anglicizations © British
and Foreign Bible Society 1997.

The Living Bible copyright © 1971 by Tyndale House Publishers.

The New Century Version copyright © 1987 by Word Publishing.

A catalogue record for this book is available from the British Library

Printed by Gutenberg Press, Tarxien, Malta

S ᴵ'ᵐ STILL STANDING

Parenting a child with a life-threatening illness

JAN BURN

FOREWORD BY DEREK J. TIDBALL

For David

*The joy, optimism, humour, courage and determination
with which you embrace each new day are a continuing
source of inspiration to me and many others whose lives
you touch. I am proud to call you my son and more
blessed by being your mother than you will ever know.*

CONTENTS

❖

FOREWORD

I wish I could put this book in the hands of every pastor.

Jan Burn has written a moving account of her experience as a mother whose young son, David, was diagnosed, without any prior warning, with cancer. With dramatic suddenness, she and her family were thrown into the unexpected world of a distant children's hospital, of chemotherapy, of blood transfusions, of hair loss—and of total uncertainty. Ten years after the traumatic events, David is still in remission, but his illness still impacts family life. Every illness, as Jan writes, brings a fresh wave of anxiety, along with the memories and emotions that she thought were dealt with long ago.

Jan has written an account that blends raw emotion with cool wisdom. She documents a range of challenges that she and her husband faced—and not just the obvious ones about suffering. How do you discipline a child who is sick—or don't you? How do you give his sisters the childhood they deserve when life revolves around their sick brother? How do you witness to other parents in an intensive care ward? She writes with transparent honesty about doctors who are pastorally inept and church members who are spiritually insensitive, and she speaks of the extra pressures involved as a result of being in pastoral ministry herself while this was all happening.

The style of this book is anything but preachy, yet it has a wonderful ability to lead us gently into various scriptures and make us see just how much God's word is relevant to even the most distressing of situations.

This is a book not just to help those who are going through similar circumstances, but one to help their friends, wider family and fellow church members to understand, so that their support can be more sensitive and their prayer more informed. Years ago, I acquired a new colleague in ministry whose daughter faced similar problems, and was treated in the same hospital as David, but without the happy ending the Burn family have so far experienced.

How I wish a book like this had been given to me then. What a difference it could have made to me and to the whole church I was pastoring at the time. The story, if not common, is frequent enough to mean that most pastors encounter it in one form or another on occasions. That's why I'd want to put this book into the hands of every pastor. I shall want to refer my students to read it, alongside works like C.S. Lewis' *A Grief Observed*, to get an understanding of the rawness of suffering.

If the title seems defeatist and less than triumphal, then read Jan's explanation of it. But think too of Paul's great prayer for the Colossians (1:11), where, having prayed for God to strengthen them with all power according to his glorious might, he says they need that strength so that they might persevere and be patient. God's strength was given to them not so that they might conquer the world or be sensational overcomers, but so that they might endure the tough experiences of life and be strong enough to go on trusting him with joy. To keep standing is sometimes the real miracle!

I trust that this book will have the wide readership it deserves.

Derek J. Tidball
Principal, London School of Theology

❖

INTRODUCTION

25 August 1993 was the day that changed my life for ever. My son David, who was seven years old, had woken up complaining of a pain in his stomach. There didn't seem anything remarkable about this at the time, since the day before he had been to a friend's birthday party and eaten too much chocolate cake! I remember saying to him that he would probably feel better by lunch-time and be well enough to go trampolining with his sister in the afternoon. That was not to be, however. The pain continued—not a severe pain, just a nagging dull ache, which by lunch-time was neither worse nor better.

Normally, I wouldn't have given it a second thought, but that day was different. I began to feel uneasy about it and made an appointment for David to see the doctor. Even as I had my hand on the telephone, making the appointment, I was tempted to change my mind. After all, I'd just be wasting his time, wouldn't I? But the uneasy feeling (which I now believe was the gentle nudging of the Holy Spirit) remained, and I will be for ever grateful that I didn't cancel that appointment.

The doctor thought David might have a grumbling appendix, and sent us to hospital to have a 'precautionary' scan. The idea that my boy could have been suffering a grumbling appendix when I'd just assumed he'd eaten too much chocolate cake seemed too awful to think about, but, oh, how many times since then I have wished it had been that simple.

The scan revealed a perfectly normal appendix and a tumour on David's kidney. I was told that the tumour was almost certainly malignant, and the image of it on the screen, invading my son's body, remains clearly etched on my mind's eye to this day. 'What do I do?' I asked the radiographer who had given me the news. In an attempt to answer my question, she told me that David and I were to be taken straight away to Bristol Children's Hospital, since our local hospital did not have the necessary specialists. But I wasn't asking, 'What *literally* do I do?' Of course, the radiographer had no reason to know this. I hardly knew what I meant myself, except that the question was much bigger than anything I had ever asked before. In those few seconds, so many thoughts never before contemplated were whirling through my mind. I felt as if I was spiralling downwards towards the deepest, darkest question I have ever faced: 'What do I do if he dies?' How does life go on without him?

David's kidney was removed and he was given six months of chemotherapy. Unfortunately, two and a half years later he relapsed. The tumour returned on his lung and he had to endure countless operations and six months of what the doctors called a 'blunder blast' second dose of chemotherapy, this time using a combination of six different drugs. David has endured a great deal of suffering during his treatment. Not only has he had to cope with the pain and trauma of operations, but also with the awful side effects of chemotherapy. Those familiar with chemotherapy will know and understand how debilitating these side effects can seem. For David, they included countless blood transfusions, mouth ulcers, hair loss, infections, nausea and severe bouts of sickness as well as general tiredness and lethargy.

A year after David relapsed, he went into remission and has remained clear of any trace of cancer for seven years now. Although the risk of a further relapse reduces with each passing year, there is no defining moment when he can be pronounced 'cured'. Children have been known to relapse eight, nine or even ten years after apparently successful treatment. Therefore, the threat of the cancer's return remains an ever-present feature of our family life. Every cough or illness brings a fresh wave of anxiety, and the memories and emotions that I thought I had successfully dealt with surface in an instant.

The past ten years have certainly been a rollercoaster ride. As a family, we have experienced tremendous highs and heartbreaking lows, through which we have learnt so much about God's love and faithfulness. The closeness of our family unit has grown immeasurably and we have learnt to value the special times together. So would I change things? I don't hesitate to answer, in a heartbeat —yes! You see, I am not one of those super-spiritual people who endure suffering quietly or patiently. I don't want my character formed during the hard times. I want God to teach me another way—a less painful way. For whatever reason, though, the path involving childhood cancer is the path along which God allowed me and my family to travel.

This book is not about my particular journey of suffering, however. As I have said, I am not very good at suffering gracefully. Anyway, a lot of books have already been written on the subject of suffering, far more moving, insightful and inspirational than I could ever write. Nor is this book an attempt to highlight the emotional and physical issues of childhood cancer *per se*. It is simply the story of a mother trying to address the unique challenges of parenting in a family with a child with a life-threatening illness. For me, it was my son's cancer. For you, it may be your daughter's cystic fibrosis or your son's muscular dystrophy or some other serious medical condition.

For those of us whose journey involves the pain and privilege of parenting in such circumstances, it can be extremely lonely. Of course, any sort of suffering is isolating, since no one can know exactly how another person feels. In my experience, however, through my son's illness and through talking to other parents in similar situations, this loneliness is made even more acute by the general lack of available resources. There are many wonderful books and organizations that exist to help bereaved parents, and I thank God for them—they do a fantastic job. There are also ever-increasing resources available on general parenting. Even so, very little help seems available to parents who, day by day, are not only called to face and live with the fear, uncertainty and stress that the life-threatening illness of their child brings, but who within such a unique situation are desperately seeking to answer their question, 'What do I do?' Perhaps, more importantly, they simply want their question to be heard—their situation acknowledged.

Of course, I would not presume to have all the answers. I am not sure I even know all the questions. To be honest, even after years of experience, I can still be taken by surprise by a situation, an event, a conversation that suddenly brings home to me in a completely different way the effect that David's illness has had on our family unit. My desire and purpose in writing this book is simply to highlight and explore some of the challenges that we, as parents in this situation, may face.

Let's also not forget to celebrate the perspective that such suffering has given us as parents, to find joy and thankfulness in the smallest of things or the most unexpected places. This was brought home to me in a new way during David's second bout of chemotherapy. At that time, the treatment didn't seem to be working and things did not look good. During this period there were some popular songs in the music charts that I found extremely painful. One such song was called 'How do I live without you?' I used to hear the words playing in a shop or petrol station and just wanted to run out as fast as I could. Anyway, one day I was out shopping with David and he suddenly stopped in the middle of the supermarket. He began jumping up and down, his little bald head swaying in time with the music. 'Listen, Mummy,' he said. 'They're playing my theme tune.' I listened and heard Elton John's 'I'm still standing' blaring out of the loudspeakers. My brave, irrepressible son was, in that moment, showing me life from a new perspective. I didn't know whether to laugh or cry, and so instead I decided to jump up and down as well. Sometimes that's just the best thing to do!

❖

Chapter 1

YEARNING FOR THE PAST

I long for the years gone by when God took care of me, when he lighted the way before me and I walked safely through the darkness.
JOB 29:2–3

As I found myself being driven to Bristol Children's Hospital, David having just been diagnosed with cancer, I experienced the first pangs of what was to become a deep longing for how life used to be. I started to think back to the beginning of that day. Life had seemed so normal. It seemed like any other day. I had done the washing and prepared the evening meal, and was looking forward to the double episode of *EastEnders* later on. I thought of the vegetables prepared in the pan on the stove and the washing hung on the line, and could not believe that it was *I*, only that same morning, just a matter of hours ago, who had done those things. Everything seemed so different now. I felt different. I thought about how, that same week, I had been anxious about the increase in mortgage rates. Now, in the light of what I had just been told, it seemed ridiculous that I had let that worry me: if only money could put this right!

That yearning for how life used to be was sometimes so overwhelming that it felt like a physical pain in the pit of my stomach. I wanted my old life back. I wanted to have normal everyday decisions to make about whether the children needed their hair cut or new shoes. I didn't want to think about red or white blood cell counts, or learn how to inject my son's anti-sickness medication. I kept thinking to myself, 'This time last week, life was good; this time last month, we were enjoying the holiday period with hardly a care in the world.' It seemed that every time I thought about the day ahead, I compared it with days and occasions before David's illness;

and often, as is the case with many people suffering the effects of trauma, I created idealized views of the past. I deeply resented the change that had been thrust upon me, but most of all I resented the fact that I had somehow lost my naivety. I was suddenly part of a world that, previously, I hardly knew existed, much less believed would ever affect my family. Of course, I'd read about such cases in women's magazines and the like, and thought, 'How tragic' and sympathized with those affected. But it never really occurred to me—not really—that something like this could ever happen to my son, to my family. Now I knew only too well that it could and it had, and somehow I needed to come to terms with this reality. An important part of accepting my 'new life' was allowing myself to grieve the loss of the past.

The need to withdraw emotionally from a sense of yearning for the past was brought home to me in a very powerful way during the course of David's relapse. David relapsed two days before we were due to go on a family holiday to Cornwall. We were going to a holiday camp, and the children were so excited about all the activities on offer. They were bitterly disappointed when they realized that we would not be able to go. I couldn't stand seeing them so devastated. It seemed so cruel that not only were they going to miss their holiday, but we'd have to spend the whole week—or weeks, as it turned out—in hospital once again. I couldn't bear to see their pain. They not only had to cope with the realization that David had cancer again, and of course this time they knew all about how awful the treatment was going to be, but they'd also missed out on their family holiday. I thought of the girls' stuff already packed in our hallway at home and desperately wanted, as most parents do, to fix it, to make it better. Before I had time to think, I said, 'Never mind, we will book to go to the same place as soon as David is well enough. You won't miss out on your holiday, I promise.'

Two years later, as soon as David was well enough, my husband and I attempted to keep that promise. True to our word, we booked a week's holiday on exactly the same site in Cornwall. We thought nothing more of it, other than that we were delighted to have made it up to them: they weren't going to miss out after all. It wasn't until we arrived at the site that we realized our mistake. You see, the children were two years older by then, and what seemed exciting to three pre-teenagers had now become very boring. Two years had passed and so had the moment for that particular holiday. Instead of grieving the loss of our holiday at the beginning, we had only delayed the inevitable. Suddenly, the realization hit me, like a brick wall, that the past two years of the children's childhood were lost for ever, and we couldn't bring them back. I couldn't fix it after all. I couldn't make up for the missing months. Time had passed, and we were all different as a result of it.

We couldn't go back; we could only go forward. We should have allowed ourselves, and the children, to grieve for that holiday and let it go. We would then have been able to enjoy a new experience with them, which was more suitable for their ages and our different circumstances. As it was, during that week we felt not only the loss of the past, but also the loss of the present. The old adage 'Time waits for no man' is true. We cannot live in the past *and* have hope for the future.

Not only that: it rained the entire week too!

One of the hardest issues to come to terms with, as parents of a child with a life-threatening illness, is how powerless it makes us feel. We cannot rescue every situation as we feel we should. We cannot always make it OK. Sometimes the situation is anything but OK, and there is absolutely nothing we can do to change it. What we can do, though, is to come to terms with the situation as it is, so that we can begin to appreciate what we have now, today. I know, as a mother, that I have shied away from this because I don't want to face the pain of what has happened. More importantly, I don't want my children to have to face the pain. As a result, I have, desperately at times, sought to protect them from the reality of the present situation, in the hope that they can somehow go through what needs to happen without realizing it. I have since come to understand that this is somewhat like King Canute sitting on the beach, trying to stop the tide coming in. The truth of it is that there is very little we can really control.

What did happen, though, was that I came to understand the good news of the gospel in a deeper way. We may realize our sense of powerlessness as parents, and that we cannot control very much around us, but it does not mean that life is out of control. In fact, in my experience, the opposite was true. I realized for the first time that when God was all I had, God was all I needed. As I sought to come to terms with the present and let go of the past, I discovered an intimacy with God that I had never before experienced.

Did this mean that the pain disappeared? No, actually it still hurts. Does it mean that I would willingly choose a future that I know will bear the scars of my son's illness? Absolutely not. I want my children to go through life carefree and pain-free, fulfilling all their dreams. Does it mean that it doesn't matter to me any more that my family has missed out on many things that I can never bring back? And I don't just mean physical things, like holidays, but emotional things, like a childhood where they are not exposed to the trauma of operations and long spells of separation from their home environment. Of course not: it mattered very much and still does. But the really amazing truth is that it also matters to God.

David, a writer of the Psalms, puts it this way: 'You keep track of all my sorrows. You have collected all my tears in your bottle. You have recorded each one in your book' (Psalm 56:8). These words are a great comfort to those who, like me, often have great difficulties facing the uncertainties of the future. We know that whatever we may face, we do so with the sure and certain knowledge that God is in control and he cares. He cares about what happens to you or me, and, most importantly for us as parents, he cares about what happens to our children. He cares about their pain and not one of their tears has gone unnoticed. In the same way, he cares about the suffering of our children.

As we seek to look forward rather than back, we can do so in the knowledge that for Christians, this life, with all its pain, is not our final destiny. Perhaps more importantly for mothers and fathers, we can do so because, as the words of a popular worship song say, our suffering children really are safe in his hands.

Forget the former things; do not dwell on the past. See, I am doing a new thing! Now it springs up; do you not perceive it? I am making a way in the desert and streams in the wasteland.

ISAIAH 43:18–19 (NIV)

❖

Chapter 2

THE CRUCIAL NATURE
OF TRUST

Better not to promise at all than to make a promise and not keep it.
ECCLESIASTES 5:5 (GNB)

As parents, my husband and I have made many mistakes during the course of our son's illness. We've been overly soft when a firmer hand was called for. We've been overly firm when a softer hand was called for. One of the biggest mistakes we made, however, concerns the area of trust. It is not that we set out deciding against telling the truth—quite the opposite: we have always been as honest as we can be with our children. It's just that sometimes, at the beginning of David's illness, we did not find out the necessary amount of truth. For example, on several occasions David was fitted with a chest drain. On the first occasion that this drain needed to be removed, David asked the doctor the question he always asked: 'Will this hurt?' (Sensible boy!) The doctor answered, 'No, I promise you won't feel a thing.'

No? It seemed rather odd to me that a tube resembling a hosepipe could be pulled from his side without hurting, but I trusted the doctor. Of course, what he should have said was, 'Yes, it will, but the pain won't last for long.' And yes, it did hurt—very much, as it turned out. I felt awful when I heard David's screams and the words, 'You promised it wouldn't hurt.' Sadly, as a result of that and other similar occurrences, David still has a mistrust of the medical profession, and, if I am honest, to a certain extent so do I. Broken trust is hard to restore.

In my attempts to be a good parent under such circumstances,

17

there were many actions that if I could turn back the clock and change, I would. Top of my list, though, is that I would take far more control, far sooner, of what was being communicated to my son. I would seek to be more informed about exactly what David could expect. For example, now I would ask the doctors, 'What will the procedure feel like? Will there be any pain? Be honest', and, 'How long is the pain or discomfort likely to last?' My regret is that I naively trusted the doctor when he told David that the removal of the drain wouldn't hurt, when all my instincts and common sense told me otherwise. I regret not following those instincts and taking the doctor aside to question him further, so that I would be in a better position to communicate the truth to David. As it was, I felt somehow tainted by the doctor's misrepresentation of how things would be. I stood there when my son looked to me for confirmation of what he was being told, and I didn't tell him the truth—not because I didn't want to, but because I didn't know. I wasn't informed enough, and I felt as if I had somehow colluded with a lie.

I am not saying that the doctor's motives were wrong. He probably thought it was the best way to get David to comply, and it worked. David did comply with what the doctor wanted on that occasion. Unfortunately, it stored up all sorts of problems for the future. From then on, David responded badly to anything the hospital staff tried to do, which in turn brought a great amount of extra and unnecessary heartache and stress, both for David and for the rest of the family. And who could blame David? After all, they had lied to him before. Why should this time be any different?

Please hear me when I say that it is not wrong, of course, to trust those who are in a position of care for our children. In any case, in many ways we have to trust those who are in such a position. I have to trust the surgeon's competence in theatre, for example, or the consultant's recommendations for treatment, since I don't have the necessary knowledge or experience to do anything other than trust that they are doing their best for my son—and I will be for ever in their debt for saving his life. In terms of what and how procedures and treatments are communicated, however, I firmly believe that, if possible, it is and should be primarily the parent's responsibility, with the support of the medics.

When we have the responsibility of care for a child with a life-threatening illness, we have to accept that we are in the situation for the long haul. It is fairly inevitable that a great deal of time will be spent going in and out of hospital. There may be all sorts of painful or uncomfortable procedures, which, as parents, we have to help our children overcome; and if we are to be successful in this task, it is absolutely crucial for our children to know that they can at least trust us. They must know that when they ask the question, 'Will it hurt?' they will get an honest answer.

I have to say that this is easier said than done. What parent wants to tell their child that something will hurt? I have often felt like scooping up my son in my arms from his hospital bed and running a million miles in the opposite direction from 'the truth'. The truth under such circumstances is often both painful and costly for the parent. In fact, sometimes it's heartbreaking, and I am quite sure that my husband, James, would say the same. For the child, though, who may face invasive procedures on a regular basis, it is freeing— they know what to expect.

Then you will know the truth, and the truth will set you free.
JOHN 8:32 (NIV)

Can you imagine the insecurity involved in waking up, every day, surrounded by unfamiliar people who are all much bigger than you, in a strange environment, often in pain, wondering what's going to happen to you today? Can you imagine then asking someone you know, 'What is going to happen?' but also knowing that you cannot trust their answer, or that they're using words that you don't recognize or understand? Imagine how out of control you would feel in that situation—how powerless.

That's what children with a life-threatening illness may face on a regular basis, and our role as parents must be to try to make some kind of sense of this strange, sometimes scary environment in which our children find themselves. We need to be translators, if you like, taking what they need to know and translating it into a language that they will understand. Of course, it is mainly the parents who are in a position to do this, since nobody knows our children as we do. No one else knows the tone of voice they best respond to, for example, or the time of day when they are most likely to receive news in the most positive way, or the words that they will understand, or what experiences they have already had that may be helpful or unhelpful in confronting whatever situation they are currently in. These things will be unique to each child. We have three children and I know that to be a good translator of truth, I need to communicate in a slightly different way with each of them. Why? Because I know them. I know their individual fears and insecurities.

As to the amount of information we divulge to our children, that is a very personal decision. We may all have slightly different ideas about how much is helpful for our children to know, and I would not presume to say what you should do in your individual situation. As a general rule of thumb, though, I tended to answer only the questions my son (and daughters, for that matter) were asking, and tell them only the things that would affect them directly. In my opinion, for example, they did not need to know statistics about survival rates for David's type of tumour. In fact, during his first course of treatment David didn't even know that cancer was life-threatening. The word 'cancer' doesn't really mean a great deal to a seven-year-old. Nor did they need to know that if the operation he was currently facing didn't work, there would be a far bigger one ahead. If they asked the question directly, however, I would feel that I had to tell them the truth—put in the most positive way I could find.

I didn't really understand just how crucial trust was until David relapsed. He had realized that his cancer had returned, and I was sitting on the steps of the hospital with him as he was trying to come to terms with the devastating news. He looked up at me, face red from crying, and said, 'Why, Mummy? Why me?' I looked into his innocent eyes, thought of all that he had already been through and all that was ahead, and felt that my heart would break. Suddenly, any well-rehearsed theologies of suffering that I had come to understand didn't seem to cut it. What could I say? 'Well, son, Eve tempted Adam with an apple and as a result we live in a fallen world full of sickness and sin.' What does that mean to a frightened ten-year-old boy? What does it mean to a frightened 36-year-old mother sitting with him, for that matter? I held him and found myself saying, 'I don't know why, love, but I do know that if I could take the tumour out of you and put it in me, I would.' His eyes lit up. 'That's exactly what Daddy has just said,' he said, and, amazingly, that was enough for David. He has never again asked 'Why?' Even now, I find this incredible, but for David it was enough that we, his parents, would have gladly taken his place. He didn't need any other explanation. He trusted us.

I have thought about this a lot over the past years and have come to realize that, as Christians, it's the same for us. We have a heavenly Father who loves us so much that he not only would take our place, but did so when he let his Son Jesus die on a cross and take on himself all the bad things in us. Where was God when I was echoing the heart's cry of my son: 'Why? Why my son?' I believe he was right there with me, on those hospital steps, holding me and saying, 'Trust me.'

'I am the good shepherd. The good shepherd lays down his life for the sheep. A hired hand will run when he sees a wolf coming. He will leave the sheep because they aren't his and he isn't their shepherd. And so the wolf attacks them and scatters the flock. The hired hand runs away because he is merely hired and has no real concern for the sheep. I am the good shepherd; I know my own sheep, and they know me, just as my Father knows me and I know the Father. And I lay down my life for the sheep.'
JOHN 10:11–15

❖

Chapter 3

LIVING WITH LONELINESS

My heart is sick, withered like grass, and I have lost my appetite. Because of my groaning, I am reduced to skin and bones. I am like an owl in the desert, like a lonely owl in a far-off wilderness. I lie awake, lonely as a solitary bird on the roof.

PSALM 102:4–7

As soon as David was diagnosed with cancer, I felt as if some invisible screen had been wrapped around me, cutting me off from the outside world. I felt as if I could see everything going on around me, but I couldn't connect with it in the same way that I once did, and it couldn't connect with me either. Even now, I feel like that to a certain extent, and it is quite isolating at times.

I was painfully aware of this sense of isolation the first time I stepped outside the hospital after David's cancer had been diagnosed. My husband had suggested that it would be good for me to get some fresh air, and I decided that since Bristol city centre was only a few minutes' walk away, I would go there. As I took my first steps outside, however, I was really taken aback by what I saw. Everyone around me was still doing exactly the same things as usual. Businessmen in suits were going to the local bar for a drink, mothers were pushing their children in buggies, a group of students were walking along, laughing and joking, and as I passed one house, the window cleaner was cleaning the windows. Shops were still open, and the sun was shining more brightly than it had done all year. I couldn't believe it! How dare these people carry on as if nothing had happened? How dare the buses keep running and the planes keep flying in the sky and, worst of all, how dare it be such a glorious day? Anger started welling up inside me. How could life be going on around me just the same as it always had?

It seems strange now to think that this was such a shock to me, but it really was. I'm not sure what I expected; I just didn't expect what I saw and heard. It seemed totally incomprehensible to me that my son was just a minute's walk away, lying in the hospital bed, my world was falling apart, and the world could go on just as before. It didn't seem to make sense. It was a bit like one of those sci-fi films in which someone journeys to a different dimension, where they can see everyone but no one can see them—a surreal feeling. But of course, that's exactly how it is. Life does go on for everyone else, even though I felt as if I were in some kind of bubble.

On that day, as I carried on walking, I was suddenly aware of a voice interrupting my thoughts, talking to me. I looked up and saw a woman shaking a tin at me, saying, 'I'm collecting for the charity CLIC (which stands for Cancer and Leukaemia In Children). Could I trouble you to give?' Can you believe that? The first person I met was collecting for a childhood cancer charity! I'm afraid any sense of irony was lost on me at the time. I just burst into tears and said, 'Sorry, I've already got one.' The woman looked completely shocked and I ran back to the hospital as fast as I could. It suddenly felt safer there. The incident amuses me now, when I think back. 'I've already got one'—what a ridiculous thing to say, and how terribly British that I would still say 'sorry'. Joking apart, though, it is true that as parents of children with a life-threatening illness, our unique circumstances and experiences do isolate us, and it can feel very lonely at times.

For one thing, our perspective on life changes. For example, when David was having many of his operations, he would be put on a surgical ward, not an oncology (cancer) ward. We would see children come in for a one- or two-day stay, have some relatively minor surgical procedure and go home, and it felt really hard to know that we would still be there the next day and the day after that, until who-knew-when. It was also hard hearing the parents of these children sharing their anxieties about what was happening, when I knew that my son's condition was life-threatening. When they complained about how difficult it was, I wanted to scream at them sometimes, 'You really don't have a clue, do you?'

I'm not saying that my attitude was fair. I'm sure I would have been the same if David had needed his appendix removing—but the point is, he didn't. He had cancer instead, and everything had changed as a result. My perspective was different. If I'm honest, it became difficult at that time to identify with and understand some-one who, from where I was now standing, had very little to worry about. At least they knew their child wasn't going to die. But it was equally hard for them to understand the depth of my fears, anxieties and pain. It seemed as if an unbridgeable gap had suddenly opened up between me and most other people, and I felt lonelier than I had ever felt in my life.

Interestingly, people responded in all sorts of different ways to the emergence of this gap. Some people, maybe because of the fear of not knowing what to say or how to behave, couldn't cope with the thought of even trying to bridge it, and simply dropped our relationship. They would avoid us when we were out and about. It was embarrassing, really, because often they were not as discreet as they thought they were. We'd see them blush red and suddenly change direction when they saw us coming.

Others had more 'spiritual' reasons not to try to bridge that gap. They were the ones who believed that, as Christians (especially as my husband and I are church pastors), we could not be walking in godly ways or with enough faith. A few people even left the church that we led because of it. This type of belief—that bad things only happen to bad people—is perhaps more common than we might think. Some people, it seems, need to apportion blame, or at least find reasons for suffering, and in some ways I can understand why. I guess they have the naive belief that standing on the 'moral high ground' offers them some sort of protection from the scary reality that this could happen to them—in their family. Speaking as a parent, however, I can confidently say that there is nothing as painful or isolating as the implication that our children's suffering is somehow our fault—as if we don't already feel full of guilt as it is.

There are also those who, with the best of intentions, try to bridge the gap but really only make the sense of isolation more acute. They try to buck us up by saying things like, 'Well, at least you've got two other children', or, 'At least you can be thankful for the seven years you have had.' Others, again probably with the best of intentions, respond by taking the 'spiritual' positive-thinking approach. I cannot count how many 'prophecies' I was given, telling me that David wouldn't need any more chemotherapy because he had been 'healed'. When I pointed out to the 'prophets' that actually the scan was still clearly showing a tumour on the screen, they would respond by saying that that didn't matter, because I had to believe 'in faith' that it was gone. But it wasn't gone! The difficulty was, of course, that once I chose to believe what I saw with my own eyes, I felt as if I had somehow let these people down. I had deprived them of their miracle, and I felt awkward with them afterwards. I certainly didn't feel free to talk about how David was doing, and neither did they. (This is not meant to imply that I am not open to hearing God speak prophetically. There have been many occasions when I have been extremely uplifted by authentic prophetic words.)

The gap is also widened by the long-term nature of many life-threatening illnesses. Other people's lives go on as normal, and this is how it should be. For those of us who—day after day, week after week, month after month, year after year—have to carry the weight of anxiety about the health and long-term future of our children, it can feel both exhausting and isolating.

This sense of isolation can also be felt between the two parents of the child, and can have a devastating effect on the marriage relationship. Over the years, I have known many relationships to collapse under the weight of pressure that parenting in such adverse circumstances brings. There are many contributing factors, a main one being that people cope with the trauma of life-threatening illness in very different ways. For example, some try to deny the seriousness of the situation, while others need to know every single detail. Some people withdraw emotionally or even shut down altogether, while others become extremely emotional and want to share their feelings in great detail and depth. Other parents find it difficult to agree with each other on the 'right' course of treatment, or the best way to communicate with their children.

Sometimes it's difficult to be in the role of both parent and partner in this situation, and we can feel that we don't have the emotional reserves to be both. Parenting in a family where there is a child with a life-threatening illness is emotionally, physically and spiritually demanding. To be honest, it is incredibly draining, and often at the end of the day we may feel we have nothing left to give: we're exhausted. Even the best relationships need an investment of time, energy and emotion, and when, month after month, one or both partners just feels empty, the relationship can come under severe strain and become very hard to get back on track.

The long-term nature of life-threatening illness means that although we may get through certain 'crisis points' in the illness, the worry and strain of it continues. As a result, it is very difficult for parents to recharge, and when the well has run dry, it takes a lot of filling. Often, we haven't even got the energy to argue and 'clear the air', and the thought of trying to summon the emotional reserves necessary to do some 'soul searching' with our partner can, at times, seem too much. It can be easier to let things slide, with each partner withdrawing more and more from the other. A sense of distance begins to emerge, and to sense this distance, this gap, emerging and to live with it—especially if it hasn't been there before—can be extremely painful. To feel separated emotionally from the very person with whom you have shared the most in the past can be one of the loneliest feelings of all.

Loneliness also develops as a result of the loss of our 'old life'. Many activities and relationships suddenly have to take second place to the responsibilities of caring for our sick child. Many parents may have to give up their paid employment, or some of their outside interests. To have such lifestyle changes thrust upon us can feel disorientating, as it means that we have to curtail many of the activities that we enjoy, that give structure to our day and reflect 'who we are'. In addition to this apparent dismantling of our old identity, we have a new identity somehow imposed on us by others. We become synonymous with our child's condition, and our identity becomes, for example, 'the mother of the child with cancer'. We find we get pitying looks from people we don't even know. I've never really known how to deal with those looks. Strangely enough, they make me want to go up to the people concerned and make it OK for *them*. I'm not quite sure why that is, but I feel as if I have somehow put a 'dampener' on their day.

It's strange, though, how you suddenly become aware that, because of your unique circumstances, people you've never met feel that in some sense they know you. Even years later, I've met people for the first time who've said things to me like, 'Of course, I know you! You're the one whose son's had cancer.' In the past, this sort of thing has made me feel overexposed and lonely, because these people don't know you at all—they know your circumstances. I found that even some of the nursing staff would add to my sense of not being a person in my own right. They would say things like, 'How are we today?' *We* always wanted to reply, 'Well, I can't speak for you, but I'm OK.' Even worse was, 'How's *mum* today?' How's mum? Don't I even have a name any more? These may sound like small issues but, for the parent who may be struggling to come to terms with such identity issues, they can add to the difficulty of trying to disentangle our own emotions and our sense of isolation.

For those of us who are Christians, perhaps one of the most painful gaps and the cause of the most intense feelings of isolation can come in our relationship with God. We may feel abandoned by God, let down by him, and may struggle to come to terms with the question, 'How could he let this happen to my child?' I had great problems, for example, with the thought that if I believed that God could heal my son in an instant (which I did and still do believe), then why didn't he? If he is a God who really loves me and doesn't want little children to suffer, why doesn't he do something? How can he sit back with all the power of the universe in his hands and do nothing? Doesn't he care? Is that any way for a loving Father to act?

Sometimes churches can add to this painful sense of isolation from God, by giving people credit for being 'spiritual' when they go through the most traumatic experience and appear to take it in their stride as if nothing has happened. These people may feel a pressure not to grieve, and not to ask the honest questions about the heart of God with which they may be struggling. That's not how the Bible tells us we have to be. The Bible doesn't say that we ought to pretend it doesn't hurt. In fact, the first step in helping us, as parents, to live with the intense pain of this special kind of loneliness is to make sure that we do just the opposite. The God of the Bible is a very big God, and he isn't the least bit threatened if I express my anger about what has happened to my son, or if you express your hurt over your child's illness.

One of the most popular books in the Bible is the book of Psalms. There are many different types of psalm, but the most common type is called the psalm of lament. These psalms ask the same sort of questions that, if we are honest, we parents want to ask: 'Why, God? How long, God? Where are you, God? Why have you hidden your face from me, God?' Many times during David's chemotherapy, Psalm 69 (which a friend of mine calls the canoeist's psalm!) seemed to sum up how I felt.

Save me, O God,
for the floodwaters are up to my neck.
Deeper and deeper I sink into the mire;
I can't find a foothold to stand on.
I am in deep water,
and the floods overwhelm me.
I am exhausted from crying for help;
my throat is parched and dry.
My eyes are swollen with weeping,
waiting for my God to help me.
PSALM 69:1–3

The truth is, not only can we tell God exactly how we feel; we need to do so if we are going to be able to process the hurt and find some comfort.

When my son was about six, before he was ill, I remember him being quite unsettled by the amount of emotion that some people were showing in church. 'Why is that man crying, Mummy?' he asked me. 'Well, love,' I said, 'it's a bit like when you've been at school all day and you've had a horrible day. Maybe your friends haven't wanted to play with you, or you've found the work difficult to understand, and you've tried to be big and brave all day. Then you see Mummy or Daddy at the school gates waiting for you, and as you run towards us you just start crying, because you know you don't have to be big and brave any more. You're safe, and you can tell us all about what a horrible day it has been and have a cuddle. It feels better then, doesn't it?' David agreed that it did. 'Well,' I said to him, 'it's just like that when grown-ups are crying in church. They're running towards their heavenly Father, and they feel safe enough to cry and tell him what a horrible day they've had, and let him make it feel better.'

What's going to break through that utter sense of loneliness inevitably felt by parents who have a child with a life-threatening illness? In my personal experience, it only happened when I made space to come into the presence of the Father, to tell him what a horrible time I'd been having, how unfair it was that I should be having it at all, and how much it hurt. How much it hurt when other children on the hospital ward went home before David. How much it hurt that some of our previous 'friends' chose to cross the street away from us, rather than have to feel uncomfortable because they didn't know what to say. How it cut like a knife having other Christians blame me for David's illness. How exhausting it felt to carry this burden day after relentless day. How much I longed to have the energy and time to spend a romantic evening with my husband. How much I missed being able to do normal things like going shopping with my friend. How confused I was about who I was becoming. How lonely it made me feel, and how much

I wanted God to sort it all out, make it go away—now! The amazing thing was that as I talked to God and told him exactly how I felt and expressed the emotion, I began to feel a peace returning, and a new strength that enabled me to think that maybe I could face another day after all.

Does this mean that the next day is going to be any less traumatic? Well, in my experience, not necessarily. Most of the time, we parents still have the same uncertainties, challenges and pain to face tomorrow that we did today. It's difficult to understand why this is so, when we've told God exactly how hard it is, but I've come to see that it's a bit like my son still having to go to school again the day after a bad day. He would often plead with me and say, 'Do I have to go to school again tomorrow, Mummy?' and, of course, I knew the answer to his question had to be, 'Yes'. There's so much more he needs to learn yet, so much more he needs to experience, and even though my heart goes out to him, I know that I wouldn't be a good parent if I held him back from all the opportunities that he needs to make him a well-rounded, mature grown-up.

In a way, I guess it's the same with us when we plead with our heavenly Father, 'Do I have to face this situation again tomorrow?' and the answer appears to be, 'Yes'. We may not like it. We may fight and scream our way to the 'school gates', but nevertheless we have to trust that there's obviously a lot more he wants us to understand yet. We've still got some growing to do. This must be the case, because God could say to us, 'No, you'll never have to go there again.' To be honest, there are many times when God's 'Yes, you *do* have to face this' makes little sense to me. It's not that I believe God caused my son to have cancer, but, for whatever reason, he allowed it and allowed it to continue. Yet here's the amazing thing: although we don't always get the answer we want to hear, God's heart goes out to us. He cares about what you and I have to go through. Not only that, but he's always there waiting at the 'school gates'—waiting for us to run into his arms, so that he can bend down and listen to what a horrible day we've had, and make us feel better. If only we would tell him!

I love the Lord because he hears
and answers my prayers.
Because he bends down and listens,
I will pray as long as I have breath!
Death had its hands around my throat;
the terrors of the grave overtook me.
I saw only trouble and sorrow.
Then I called on the name of the Lord:
'Please, Lord, save me!'
How kind the Lord is! How good he is!
So merciful, this God of ours!
The Lord protects those of childlike faith;
I was facing death, and then he saved me.
Now I can rest again,
for the Lord has been so good to me.

PSALM 116:1–7

❖

Chapter 4

LEARNING TO BE FLEXIBLE

Hope deferred makes the heart sick, but when dreams come true, there is life and joy.
PROVERBS 13:12

When our son was first diagnosed with cancer, we were totally unprepared for how intrusive his illness would be in all aspects of life. I can remember being bitterly disappointed on lots of occasions when the plans for family celebrations, such as Christmas or birthdays or anniversaries, had to be curtailed as David developed an infection or needed a blood transfusion. It was hard on the whole family, as we have always looked forward to such occasions with great excitement, and, as a parent, I found it especially painful. I found it hard to cope not only with my own sense of disappointment, but also with the disappointment of my two girls, and hard then to find the inner strength to provide the reassurance and comfort that David needed as he faced the next bout of ill health. It was difficult to remain optimistic: as if this cancer hadn't taken enough away from our family already, it was also denying us the opportunity to have anything positive to look forward to. For a period of time, it seemed to bulldoze to the ground everything good we tried to build. It was hard to come to terms with all those lost opportunities. I suppose that, in the grand scheme of things, they shouldn't have mattered compared with David's long-term well-being, but they did matter. They mattered very much. It mattered that when Katie (our eldest daughter) had her first day at senior school, I hadn't slept for many nights and was so tired that it all passed in a bit of a blur. It mattered that so many of our traditional family Saturday nights in, with pizza and a video or TV, had to be cancelled.

The problem was that every time we had to cancel something special planned for the family, it piled on the pressure for the next event to 'really work'. I felt the stress of the mounting pressure to make up for these 'lost occasions' so that all three of the children wouldn't feel that they'd missed out on something special. Days or weeks before one of the children's birthdays, I would plead with God for David to be well, or at least well enough to be home; and when he wasn't, as was so often the case, I felt devastated. It really did make my 'heart sick'. It was only through the process of cancelling event after event that I realized how living like this, with disappointment after disappointment, just brought more heartache. Something had to change. Eventually, my husband and I decided that we needed to be much more spontaneous and flexible in our approach to family life. We decided, for example, that in our family we would all be like the Queen and have an 'official' birthday when we would give presents and celebrate together at a time that suited us—a time when David was well enough and the whole family could be together.

As you are reading this, you may be thinking, 'That's no great insight. It's obvious—just change the day.' But for many of us struggling to come to terms with the enormous changes that life-threatening illness brings, it's not so simple, and we find ourselves desperately trying to cling on to whatever bits we can of our past family life. There are many different reasons for this, but one in particular is that it is scary to accept that we may have to adopt a new approach to nearly all our routines. We may believe that if we can still do the same things together as a family that we always did, in the way that we always did them, then maybe life isn't as out of control as we fear it is. At an even deeper emotional level, we may feel that if we accept that all aspects of our lives are thrown up in the air, then somehow the illness has won. It has successfully invaded everything. In consequence, we try to make the illness fit around our plans rather than accepting the inevitable, which is that we have to learn to fit our plans around it.

It's a bit like parents who are expecting their first baby saying,

'Our life isn't going to change when we have our baby. We're still going to be doing exactly the same things that we always did and be just the same people.' Those of us who already have children think to ourselves, 'Yeah, right! They'll find out soon enough that it won't be that simple.' Why? Because we know from experience that they have not yet faced the reality of how disruptive and all-consuming one little person can be. They are thinking in terms of the ideal and not the real. In a similar way, we parents of children with a life-threatening illness need at some stage to face the reality of our situation, and not try to make it conform to how we would choose it to be ideally.

Lord, grant me the grace to accept the things I cannot change,
The courage to change the things I can,
And the wisdom to know the difference.
'SERENITY PRAYER' BY REINHOLD NIEBUHR

Facing the reality of our situation doesn't mean, though, that we need to be pessimistic, give in, or always expect the worst. It just means that we need to accept the fact that there are some things we can't change: they're bigger than we are. For example, we couldn't change the fact that David needed regular blood transfusions when his red blood cell count dropped too low. Nor could we 'diary it in'. It happened when it happened, and that was that. All my efforts to 'will' it to be different left me even more anxious and exhausted. At a time when there is already far too much stress and anxiety around, we parents need to choose carefully what we are going to hold on to and what we are going to let go. This doesn't mean that we can't look forward to having fun together: we need to hold on tightly to the value of such family times. But we do need to be more relaxed about the importance of when those times happen. In holding lightly to the 'when', we protect ourselves and our children from much potential disappointment.

David's illness showed me in many ways that I wasn't as 'in control' as I thought I was. I couldn't make everything happen according to my plan or my schedule, and, like many of us when something concerns the well-being of our children, I fought hard against the sense of powerlessness and vulnerability that it brought about. Amazingly, though, the smaller I saw myself and the more I admitted my own limitations, the bigger I began to see God. The less trust I had in my ability to 'make things better', the more I had to depend upon God and trust that he really was in control. Then I found that God began to give me the grace to accept what I couldn't change—accept the situation as it really was.

'Lord, to whom would we go? You alone have the words that give eternal life.'
JOHN 6:68

Speaking personally, I have found that learning to be more flexible and spontaneous in my approach to parenting has been an enriching and positive experience. I have been able to 'seize the day' far more than I ever did before David was ill. I have gained a fresh appreciation of the preciousness of the moment, enjoying it simply because it's there. I can remember one occasion, for example, when it started snowing late one evening, when the children were already in bed. Before David was ill, I might have thought, 'I hope the snow doesn't melt, because they'll enjoy seeing it in the morning, but it's too much effort to get them up now.' But nothing changes your perspective like a threat to the life of someone you love, and straight away I found myself thinking, 'So what if it's late? The snow might not be there tomorrow, and, if it is, David might not be well enough to go out in it.' So my husband and I got the children up out of their beds. There and then, we all went outside and felt the cold wet snow falling on our faces. It was a magical moment that I wouldn't have missed for the world—not now!

Look here, you people who say, 'Today or tomorrow we are going to a certain town and will stay there a year. We will do business there and make a profit.' How do you know what will happen tomorrow? For your life is like the morning fog—it's here a little while, then it's gone. What you ought to say is, 'If the Lord wants us to, we will live and do this or that.' Otherwise you will be boasting about your own plans, and all such boasting is evil.

JAMES 4:13–16

❖

Chapter 5

LEARNING TO LISTEN

My dear brothers and sisters, be quick to listen, slow to speak, and slow to get angry.
JAMES 1:19

One of the most difficult things for parents is to watch our children go through any sort of emotional pain. I can remember when Katie was in junior school and had two best friends. Most of the time, those relationships worked out fine, but every now and again the other two girls would pair up and exclude Katie from what they were doing, and she would come home devastated by their rejection of her. I knew that this was something that young girls in three-somes tend to do, and that, no doubt, they would be back to normal the next day. Even so, I think I sometimes felt more upset by it than Katie did. I wanted to go straight round to see the girls' mothers and tell them just what kind of daughters they had. I used to rehearse the conversation in my head and work out all the different scenarios. 'Well,' I'd think, 'if she says *this*… I'll say *that*… And if she says *that*… I'll say *this*… and just let her try and bring up the "sweets incident". Then she'll really be told a few home truths about her daughter.'

Of course I didn't go through with it, mainly (I have to confess) because of the restraint and wisdom of James. It's hard, though, to have to let our children go through that kind of pain, and what has caused me the most heartache as a parent has been watching the emotional pain that David's cancer has caused all three of our children. When pain is physical, we parents generally feel much more able to comfort our children. It's easier to see and understand, for one thing, and we can 'kiss it better' or put a 'special cream' on it. Emotional pain is often a different story, and there is a great deal of emotional pain attached to life-threatening illness. We can't see it or touch it; it often produces responses in our children that are very painful to see; and, as parents, we usually bear the brunt of such responses since we are the closest to them. David, for example, would have long spells of not communicating with us. This was completely out of character for him, as he was and still is a very communicative person. He has always wanted to tell us every little detail about his day, yet suddenly he had long periods of being withdrawn and silent, and I found it intensely painful to feel that I could not reach my son emotionally.

It wasn't that David chose not to communicate with me only: he withdrew from just about everybody. There was one person that he would talk to, though—Sue (not her real name), who was a play specialist employed by the hospital to work with sick children. Sue had an amazing gift of being able to communicate with children, and they all loved her and responded positively to her. To be honest, I felt a little jealous of her at first: she could get through to my son when I couldn't. It's hard to accept that sometimes our children need other people as well as us.

What was it about Sue that made her so special? Well, after hours of being with her, I came to the conclusion that it was simply because she listened. I don't just mean that she heard what the children said—she did so much more than that. She gave them her full, undivided attention. Sue would always communicate with the children at a level where eye contact could be made, and if this meant lying on the floor with them, she would lie on the floor. She managed to make the children feel that at that moment in time, nothing and no one was more important than they were, and she was ruthlessly single-minded in this. I once saw her in conversation with David when a consultant came and tried to interrupt them. He assumed that his time with her was obviously more important than David's, and that what he had to say was undoubtedly of greater significance than anything David was sharing. Sue didn't think so, however, and would have none of it.

She didn't even glance at the consultant, but kept her eyes firmly fixed on David the whole time, and held up her hand to show the consultant that she was busy.

I found this highly amusing, since most consultants aren't used to being told what to do. I admired Sue very much for putting my son's needs above anyone else's and was delighted at the level of respect she had accorded him—delighted, that is, until one day she did exactly the same thing to me, and I got the 'hand treatment'! Some thought had occurred to me, and I just blurted it out, unaware that David was talking to her. When she signalled me to stop, I have to say that I felt slightly indignant. My pride was more than a little damaged, mainly, I think, because I recognized that she was right. I should have been more respectful to them both. When she and David had finished their conversation, Sue then turned to me, said, 'What was it that you wanted to talk to me about?' and gave me the same focused attention that she had given my son. Mind you, I wasn't that gracious. I was still sulking, and simply muttered, 'I can't remember now!'

I learnt a lot from Sue about the tremendous power of listening— I mean really listening. When we give someone our full attention, we're communicating so much to them. We're saying, 'You're worth it, and right now nothing matters more than you.' We give them dignity and respect, and for children who have a life-threatening illness this is so important and healing. They are used to being prodded and poked, having strangers standing at the end of their hospital bed and discussing them as if they weren't there. Many things in hospital life can serve to strip them of their self-respect and dignity, leaving them feeling disempowered, and they desperately need to know that their opinion does matter. They need to feel that they have been heard, that they have a voice.

If listening to someone—giving them our full, undivided attention—is so healing, why do most of us find it difficult? Well, there are lots of reasons. In today's high-tech, fast-paced society, we are not in the habit of concentrating on one thing or one person for long. Our minds start wandering, as any preacher will tell you!

Most of us are also quite selfish, and we would much rather have someone listening to us.

For those of us whose child has a life-threatening illness, there are other more painful reasons, the main one being that we're scared of what we might hear. Children have a unique ability to get bluntly to the heart of an issue, and we can never be quite certain what they might say—it's a risk. Most of the time it doesn't matter, as the things they come out with are amusing—or, at worst, slightly embarrassing, such as when they decide to talk about our family secrets in public. But when we face the trauma of a threat to life, it's a whole different story: there's a lot more at stake. If we allow our children to be *really* honest, will we, as parents, be able to cope? What might they or their brothers and sisters say? What might they ask? Will they speak out loud my darkest unspoken fear? Will they ask, 'Will I die?' What if I get out of my depth with them? What if I can't cope? What if I break down in front of them?

You see, when we really listen to our children, the big risk and fear is about what they might say. To avoid this, we tend to try to keep things on an even keel, keep it positive, keep it light. Why? Because that's how *we* need it to be; that's what *we* can cope with. There are days when all we can cope with is getting up and facing another day, and that's OK. We're not superhuman: we're just ordinary people—parents doing the best we can in the face of the unthinkable. There are times, though, when we parents do need to pay the price of listening to our children—and make no mistake, there is a price to pay. To give anyone our full attention, to be fully present emotionally, can be totally draining. When the person whom we hear describing their pain and confusion is our child, it cuts like a knife through our heart. The amazing thing, though, is that this act of listening also takes our understanding of and relationship with our son or daughter to new depths.

How do we, as parents, find in the midst of our own pain the emotional energy we need really to listen to our child? When we are full to the brim with hurt and fears ourselves, how can we trust ourselves not to project those feelings on to our child and make the child feel worse than they already do? I can remember times when I felt so full of pain that I was almost scared to breathe. It felt as if, with one false move, I would collapse in a sobbing heap on the floor. What do we do in those times? How do we find not only the strength to go on but also the strength to give all the emotional support our children need?

We only find the resources and comfort we need to cope by being listened to ourselves. Actually, we have the same need for someone else's undivided attention that our children have. We have the same need to be heard. We have the same need to be treated with dignity and respect, the same need to voice our darkest fears and ask the questions that haunt us. We need to know that we matter.

I have been very fortunate in that I have James and a couple of really close friends who have listened to me, and have paid the emotional price of 'being there' for me, and for that I will be for ever grateful. But just as we are only human, so are our listeners and supporters. They have their own pain to process and their own commitments to fulfil, and, as much as they might want to, they cannot be emotionally available to us 24 hours a day. What happens when they can't be there, or when, try as they might, they just haven't got the energy or under-standing truly to hear what we are saying? Or what happens when we fear that the burden we are carrying is too great to place on someone else, when it doesn't seem fair to them? I have discovered the incred-ible truth that in these circumstances God pays attention to us. This is one reason why writers of the Bible speak so often of God's face.

The Lord bless you and keep you; the Lord make his face to shine upon you and be gracious to you; the Lord turn his face toward you and give you peace.
NUMBERS 6:24–26 (NIV)

This is the blessing that God himself taught the people of Israel. To turn your face towards someone is to give that person your full attention. When we do this, we are not listening casually, our mind preoccupied with other thoughts or our heart distracted by whatever else is happening around us. We are saying, 'I'm fully, emotionally present.' This is the kind of attention that God lavishes on us.

It gets even better, however. This blessing says that God will not only turn his face towards us; he will also make it shine on us. The shining face is a picture of wonder and joy. Our faces shine only when we're in the presence of those whom we love most deeply, and this, says the blessing, is how God loves us. The God of the Bible is a God who notices, who longs to give us his full, undivided attention, who hears us—and if that means being down on the floor with us as we've collapsed in that sobbing heap, then so be it!

As parents of a child with a life-threatening illness, one of the hardest things to cope with is the fact that we can't take it away from them: we can't take away their physical pain. By learning to listen, however, we can bear the weight of, and help them process, the emotional pain that they carry. To do this under such circumstances is costly—it really is. We may have to hear things from our children that we never imagined we would have to hear, even in our worst nightmares, and it's scary. They may tell us how frightened they are about dying, or how scared they are about having to leave the rest of the family behind if they die. When David was in hospital, he would often speak of his longing to be home and to have his old life back, and listening to him describing his heartfelt desires at those times was extremely painful for James and me. 'I just want my own quilt and my own bed,' he'd cry. 'I want to play tennis in the garden with Katie and Hannah, like I used to. I don't want any more operations or chemotherapy or hospital food. I want you just to take me home, Mummy, and I want Daddy to tell the doctors, "David isn't coming back here any more."' I would find it heart-rending to have to listen to his cries.

Such intensity of emotion is exhausting, and if we are to have the emotional strength to keep on listening to our children, week after week, month after month or even year after year, our own cries need to be heard. As a Christian, one of the most amazing lessons I have learnt is that our cries really are heard, and there's not the smallest detail of our life that's not of immense interest to God.

O Lord, you have searched me and you know me.
PSALM 139:1 (NIV)

Do you realize that right now, as you read this, you have the full attention of the God who made the universe? What an awesome thought, that God is listening to you! I wonder what you might want to say to him.

In my distress I called to the Lord; I cried to my God for help. From his temple he heard my voice; my cry came before him, into his ears.
PSALM 18:6–8 (NIV)

❖

Chapter 6

DISCOVERING THE HEALING POWER OF FORGIVENESS

Jesus said, 'Father, forgive them, for they do not know what they are doing.'
LUKE 23:34 (NIV)

As a parent of a child with a life-threatening illness, I know both from my own experience and from speaking to many other parents in a similar position that sooner or later (and it's probably going to be sooner) there will be situations arising from our unique circumstances that force us to choose between forgiveness and revenge. Doctors may make mistakes, for example; friends may turn their backs on us; schools may not be helpful in accommodating our child's specific needs. These are just some of the issues with which we may have to cope on a regular basis, and they have the capacity to produce strong emotion in us, causing us to feel both pain and anger.

When my son was first diagnosed with cancer, it was a complete shock. He had gone into hospital to have a precautionary scan for a suspected grumbling appendix, and we were expecting to go home straight afterwards. As it turned out, we didn't return home until weeks later, by which time David was minus one kidney, had had countless tests, and had completed his first course of chemo-therapy. The suddenness with which it all happened was very traumatic, but it was made even more so by a series of administrative errors, which meant that information was not communicated as well as it should have been. I have no desire to speak negatively about the medical profession—as I have said, they saved my son's life—but there were also times when, in all honesty, they added to my pain.

When David's cancer was first diagnosed, for example, I was sent straight away to Bristol Children's Hospital with a huge brown envelope containing his scan results. Until this point, all I had been told was that David had a tumour on his kidney, almost certain to be malignant, and that there might be another tumour in his stomach. When I pleaded with the staff to tell me more, I was told that I'd have to wait until the scan was looked at by a consultant in Bristol. So I arrived at Bristol, envelope in hand, desperate for someone to talk to, to tell me what it all meant. First, David and I had to wait two and a half hours in the accident department, sitting on a trolley, before anyone came to see us. Eventually, a doctor arrived. Thank goodness, at last someone would be able to give me some answers and, I hoped, some reassurance. I eagerly handed him the envelope containing the scan results for him to examine. He reached his hand deep inside, and guess what? They weren't there! The envelope was empty. Someone had obviously forgotten to put them in. Nothing more could be done that evening because, as the doctor told me, 'David can't be fitted in for another scan, and it isn't worth sending a taxi to Gloucester from Bristol to collect the original scan results.'

I was absolutely gutted. How could they have been so careless as not to include David's scan results? And how could they say it wasn't 'worth' putting this mistake right tonight—now—so that at least my family could have something to begin to make sense of. 'Isn't worth it for whom?' I wondered. The results were ready, yet here I was, facing a whole night and half a day with no news of them. It was one of the longest nights of my life. To have only the worst kind of news, with no more details, was torture, intensified by my continually visualizing the scan images sitting on someone's desk. They were lying somewhere, and held the key to many of the answers I craved. Over the years, there were many more such instances, and with each one I found it more difficult not to feel bitter.

It was also hard not to feel bitter towards friends who just seemed to disappear when the going got tough. I felt so let down by them. Hadn't we once said that we would always be there for each other? Hadn't I stood by them during their difficult times? It was even more difficult not to let the feelings of betrayal by other Christians, who sought to blame me and my husband for David's illness, sow seeds of resentment in our lives. After all, that sort of betrayal is devastating.

If an enemy were insulting me,
I could endure it.
If a foe were raising himself against me,
I could hide from him.
But it is you, a man like myself,
my companion, my close friend,
with whom I once enjoyed sweet fellowship
as we walked with the throng at the house of God.
PSALM 55:12–14 (NIV)

As we face the task of parenting under such circumstances, it seems almost inevitable that we will have to cope with responses from other people that may be a source of pain. We may have to face people's lack of understanding, for example, or their judgmental attitudes, or their carelessness, and the intensity of the hurt caused by some of these attitudes is not to be underestimated. We're already coping with just about all we feel we can handle, and when people who we feel should know better appear to choose, for whatever reason, to add to the pain of our situation, it can be devastating. It is also often the case that we don't have the time and opportunity to process the emotions that such responses from other people can bring, so we tend to bury the hurt and anger. The problem is, though, that we don't bury pain dead; we bury it alive. Sooner or later it surfaces, often in inappropriate or damaging ways, such as uncontrollable angry outbursts, depression, resentment or self-pity.

What's the answer? How do we deal with such 'offences' from other people, so that we don't end up being consumed or destroyed by them? How do we protect ourselves from bitterness taking root in our lives? The answer is simple, really: we need to choose to forgive. Is this difficult? Absolutely! It's hard enough forgiving people whose actions have hurt us personally, but when their actions have hurt and affected our children, it's an altogether different story. As a mother, I know I want to flatten anyone who hurts my children. Often the last thing I want to do is forgive them. I want them to pay, and pay big-time! But the truth is that if we are going to walk through the experience of the long-term illness of our child and remain as 'whole' as possible, we have no choice but to forgive. Likewise, if we want our children to remain as physically, spiritually and emotionally whole as possible in the face of such suffering and adversity, we need to be modelling in our lives the freedom that forgiveness brings.

When we choose to forgive, God can start the process of healing in our life. He can heal us from the pain of what's happened and give us a new hope for the future.

As I said, however, forgiveness isn't easy, especially in the face of a life-threatening illness. Sometimes it's made harder by our false understanding of what forgiveness is, and what it isn't. We may feel that we can't forgive because it hurts too much. But the first step towards walking in forgiveness doesn't involve our emotions—how we feel: it involves our will. We need to make a choice to forgive. If we wait until we feel like forgiving, we may wait for ever. Sometimes we find it hard to forgive because we feel that, in making the choice to forgive, we're somehow trivializing what happened, or saying that what happened no longer matters, but that's just not true. It still matters very much. It matters to us, and it matters to God. What we are saying is that we are choosing to release that person, or those people, from our judgment into God's judgment. Of course, God has given us free will, and you and I don't have to do this: it's our choice.

Whatever choice we make, we need to bear in mind the wise

words of someone who said, 'Unforgiveness is the cancer of the human soul.' Unforgiveness locks us into the prison of the past. It drives us to nurse and rehearse grudges and grievances until eventually everything we see is coloured by the lenses of bitterness and resentment. If we choose to continue being consumed by thoughts of getting even, or bitterness at what's been done to us, we will find that it's not only our child's body that is damaged by their illness; it's also the emotional and spiritual well-being of the whole family.

I can understand that this might sound like a rather extreme statement, especially if, like me, you have witnessed first-hand the way cancer can ravage a body. I have also seen first-hand how unforgiveness and bitterness can ravage a family, though, and I have honestly found this to be more alarming and distressing. The truth is that harbouring resentment and bitterness towards someone, or some people, is like dying a slow death. Unforgiveness destroys so much. It kills our sense of optimism or our ability to trust someone completely again. It can make us so consumed with the idea of getting even that we can't think of anything else. It can rob us of our sense of peace with God, and it really doesn't provide the firm foundation on which to build a secure and happy family life.

They have planted the wind and will harvest the whirlwind.
HOSEA 8:7a

The need to be walking in forgiveness continually, to keep making the choice to forgive when we've been let down time after time, has been one of my biggest personal battles in fighting my son's illness. There have been times when even to make a choice to forgive, to make a decision of my will to let something go, has not been easy. There have also been times when I have made that choice— expressed the pain of the particular hurt that someone has caused me or my family—and yet still felt a fresh rush of pain and anger when I have seen them again. Does this mean that I hadn't truly forgiven them the first time? Not necessarily. It can mean that a fresh layer of hurt has risen to the surface, and I need to choose to forgive and allow God to heal me again. I have heard it said that we're onions, not oranges—we have many layers—and this can certainly be true in the area of forgiveness. As a fresh layer of hurt comes to the surface, we need to choose to forgive again; and as another layer surfaces, we need to choose to forgive again and again. At last, one day we meet the person who has hurt us, and although we still have the memory of what's happened, we do not have the anger or pain attached to it, which is an incredibly liberating feeling.

This was the issue that Jesus was addressing with Peter, when he asked Jesus, 'Lord, how many times shall I forgive my brother when he sins against me? Up to seven times?' Jesus answered, 'I tell you, not seven times, but seventy times seven' (Matthew 18:21–22, NIV). Jesus didn't mean we should forgive 490 times (if you're good at maths). He meant, 'Don't count': 'seventy times seven' is a Jewish phrase that means 'millions'.

This can mean choosing to forgive a person repeatedly for many different things that they have done to hurt us, or it can mean that we have to continue forgiving someone for the same thing that they have done over and over again. Forgiveness can have layers. There may be depths of forgiveness to which we have to go. That's not easy, is it, when we've been hurt deeply? Especially if the other person doesn't even acknowledge what they've done. The truth is that our forgiveness of them is not dependent upon their saying 'sorry'; it's unconditional.

I must be honest and say that, as a Christian, I have struggled with the unconditional nature of forgiveness. I could accept, in a way, that many friends couldn't seem to understand what I was going through. I thought back to my own understanding—or rather, lack of it—before David's cancer was diagnosed, and I could understand why they responded as they did. This was, after all, completely outside their experience. How could they know what it was like? I could even understand the fear that would sometimes motivate people to reject my family. In these situations, I wouldn't say it was easy, but I could pray with Jesus, 'Father, forgive these people, because they don't know what they are doing' (Luke 23:34).

However, the greatest difficulty I had in choosing to forgive concerned the carelessness with which some people in the medical profession treated David. Thankfully, many medics gave David a very high level of care, for which I remain eternally grateful. But, for example, there were those who would 'forget' test results, and others who didn't monitor David's rising temperature, resulting in his suffering more than was necessary. Of course, I could have understood if the staff were needed elsewhere—we're all aware of how stretched the NHS budget is—but sometimes that just wasn't the case. On one occasion, some nurses who were supposed to be overseeing David's treatment were talking about their social night out rather than giving him his anti-sickness medication on time. Worse still, when, as a result of their inaction, they saw David violently vomiting, they showed no remorse. In these sorts of situations, I found it hard to pray, 'Father, forgive them, for they don't know what they are doing.' Wasn't it obvious that they knew what they were doing? The fact that they still didn't see and take responsibility for the consequences of their actions, though, had nothing to do with the choice that I had to make to forgive. Forgiveness, like God's love for us, is unconditional.

When we were utterly helpless, Christ came at just the right time and died for us sinners. Now, no one is likely to die for a good person, though someone might be willing to die for a person who is especially good. But God showed his great love for us by sending Christ to die for us while we were still sinners.

ROMANS 5:6–8

It isn't just other people that we, as parents of a child with a life-threatening illness, can find difficult to forgive. Some of us may need to take the courageous step of 'forgiving' God. I realize that, theologically, since God cannot sin, we will never really have anything to forgive God for, but there are times when it doesn't feel like that, and we blame God for things that are not his responsibility. We can see this happening in 2 Kings 6:33: 'While Elisha was still saying this, the messenger arrived. And the king said, "It is the Lord who has brought this trouble on us! Why should I wait any longer for the Lord?"'

The hospital environment, particularly the intensive care unit or a high-dependency ward in a children's hospital, is a unique environment in that it is a great leveller. No matter what background the people around us have, we know that we are all struggling with the same thing—the serious illness of our child. Although we may each choose to express it and deal with it differently, we share the pain of the utter helplessness we feel as parents, seeing our children so ill. It's amazing how, in this environment, emotions are often laid bare—how we can find ourselves, in the space of just a few hours, sharing the most personal details of our lives with a virtual stranger. We share details that, under normal circumstances, may require years of establishing a trusting relationship before they are disclosed.

I was having one such heart-to-heart with a woman whom we will call Jane. She and I had shed many tears together, and we both felt a tremendous sense of affinity for one another, since both our sons had cancer—right up to the time, that is, when she discovered that my husband and I were pastors of a church. Then she suddenly became extremely angry. 'How can you possibly believe in a God that would do this to my son?' she yelled. 'Let me tell you a few things about your God.' She went on to explain how, ever since they were married, she and her husband had desperately longed for children. After 17 years and all sorts of painful and embarrassing infertility treatment, she eventually conceived their son. They were delighted, thanking God for the miracle he had given them, right up until the moment he was born and it was discovered that he had Down's syndrome. Their son was three before she felt that she had come to terms with what had happened, and four when he was diagnosed with leukaemia. 'Now you tell me,' she said, 'how you can possibly talk about a God who would do that to us?'

What could I say? I don't think I could have said anything had it not been for the fact that we both knew that my son was, at the time, in a far more critical condition than hers. Somehow I felt that this gave me the credibility to talk about my God, who I knew had not caused my son's or her son's illness. Although it was difficult, I had to be honest with her about the confusion I felt over the fact that God was allowing my family to go through this trauma. Sometimes as Christians, and perhaps especially as church leaders, we feel we have to be spin doctors for God. When things don't seem to go well, or are outside our own understanding, we feel obliged to do some sort of cover-up job, to let God 'off the hook'. We fear that by saying, 'I don't know all the answers' or admitting that we're struggling too, we won't be a 'good witness'. Increasingly, however, in my experience, people don't want answers as much as they want honesty—to know that they can trust what we say.

Talking to Jane that day, I felt like the blind man whom Jesus healed, who said, 'Whether he is a sinner or not, I don't know. One thing I do know. I was blind but now I see!' (John 9:25, NIV). I had never before been so acutely aware of all that I didn't know. Never had I been so aware of all the questions for which I didn't have, and would probably never have, the answers. And yet—here's the amazing thing—I had also never been so sure that my God's heart was breaking for no one more than it was breaking for Jane's that day. I had never been so aware that he desperately wanted to lavish on her all the comfort and love he had shown to me.

I would love to say that Jane immediately fell to her knees, said sorry to God that she had held him in her judgment, and invited the Lord Jesus Christ into her life, but sadly it wasn't like that. Jane was so full of unforgiveness towards God that I'm not really sure how much she heard at that moment. I haven't seen Jane for years, but I do think of her from time to time, and pray that if she hasn't done so already, she would be able to choose to stop blaming God for things that aren't his responsibility. I pray that she would be freed from her dark, hopeless, cold prison of unforgiveness, and would begin to experience the warmth of God's healing and restoring love as she faces the future—whatever that holds.

It's not easy to forgive those who we feel have hurt us. It's even more difficult forgiving those who have hurt our children. In all honesty, however, perhaps the person whom I have had the most constant ongoing difficulty in forgiving has been myself.

❖

Chapter 7

FINDING FREEDOM FROM GUILT

'All I want is a reasonable answer—then I will keep quiet. Tell me, what have I done wrong?'
JOB 6:24

In my role as pastor of a local church, I lead parenting courses for the people in the surrounding community. As I lead these courses, I have noticed that there tends to be a common theme that unites us as parents, whatever our backgrounds: to one extent or another, most of us feel a sense of guilt. It always strikes me as somewhat ironic, really, since these people see their role as parents as having enough importance and value to merit giving up six precious evenings of their time to attend a parenting course, yet they still feel guilty that they're somehow 'not good enough'. I have seen parents on such courses who are great parents and doing their very best, but are still breaking their hearts because of the sense of guilt they carry about their parenting abilities. I have long since arrived at the conclusion that guilt comes with the territory of being parents!

When we have a child with a life-threatening illness, there's a real danger of letting feelings of guilt get completely out of proportion. One reason for this is that, as parents, we feel it's our role to protect our children—and in many ways it is. There are some things, though, that we just cannot protect our children from—my son's cancer being an example. Of course, with our heads we know this is true, but the problem is that our hearts often tell us something different, and we become extremely vulnerable to taking on board a load of false guilt.

The heart is deceitful above all things and beyond cure. Who can understand it?
JEREMIAH 17:9 (NIV)

We can start blaming ourselves for all sorts of things over which, in reality, we had little or no control. For example, although I know in my head that I took David to the doctor the very first time that he displayed any symptoms of his cancer, my heart tells me that somehow, as his mother, I should have instinctively known the instant when those first few cancer cells formed together to become a tumour. How could I have not known? How could I have carried on as normal when that 'thing' must have already been invading his body? How could I have been so stupid?

As David went through his treatment, there were a hundred and one things that I felt guilty about. I felt guilty that I couldn't spend enough time with Katie and Hannah. I felt guilty that when I did spend time with them, I had very little emotional or physical energy to give to them, when they deserved so much more. I felt guilty that, at times, I hardly saw my husband and couldn't support him in his ministry as much as I wanted to. I felt guilty when other parents of children in a similar situation were being told that there was no hope. My son was still being treated, yet they were facing the imminent loss of their child. I felt guilty that my husband shouldered so much of the burden of my pain. I felt guilty for all the times I hadn't been as patient with David, or with Hannah or Katie, as I might have been.

Guilt, it seemed, was ready to ambush me from even the most unexpected places. One of my worst episodes of guilt came as a result of taking part in a survey. I was approached by an organization doing some research into various possible links to childhood cancer. A representative from the organization requested a meeting with me to ask some basic questions about lifestyle and family background and so on. The last thing I wanted to do at the time was to have to answer any more questions about my son's illness, but I felt a certain moral obligation to do so: it seemed a small sacrifice to make if it helped to prevent other children from going through what David had endured. Anyway, even though I wasn't looking forward to the meeting, I was totally unprepared for just how emotionally drained and full of guilt it would leave me feeling.

The meeting lasted for two hours, and seemed to cover every detail of my life, including the more obvious things such as family medical history, down to the smallest details such as the brand of washing powder I used. Some of these questions were difficult to answer; some were simply tedious. However, one question in particular haunted me for years afterwards, and it was, 'Have you ever had your hair highlighted?' I replied, 'Yes, regularly.' The next question was whether I had any objection to my hairdresser being contacted in order to ascertain the name of the specific brand of hair dye used. I said I didn't mind, but the fact that they thought this information significant enough to make it worth contacting my hairdresser made my stomach churn and my legs go weak. 'They must know more about this than they're letting on,' I thought, and within a couple of seconds I had developed some sort of conspiracy theory. 'They must have a lot of evidence that mothers using hair dye are somehow responsible for their child's cancer,' I concluded, and of course you can guess where this chain of thought took me next. Suddenly I was convinced that scientific evidence existed to confirm that my son's illness *really was my fault*.

As I write this now, from the perspective of a great deal of healing and the passing of time, I can appreciate how illogical and over-the-top my thought process was. At the time, though, it didn't seem that way at all. I left that meeting eaten up with the belief that if only I hadn't been so vain, and had accepted that God intended me to be mousy and not a blonde bombshell, then my son would still be OK. Although it now seems slightly amusing, it took a long time for that thought to leave me completely, and the associated false guilt caused me a great deal of heartache.

It's not just mothers who are prone to feelings of guilt. My husband James talks of his sense of guilt about the times when David was in hospital. Having two other children meant that one of us usually took care of them at home while the other stayed with David in hospital. It generally worked out that I stayed with David while James looked after our girls. Of course, James would come to see David and me, but in order to do so, he had to drive 40 miles along a stretch of motorway linking our home with the hospital where David had all his operations. He says that whatever direction he was travelling in along that stretch of road, he would feel that he was going the wrong way. He would feel guilty about leaving the girls to drive to the hospital to see David and me, and then feel guilty about leaving the hospital to drive home to be with our girls. Even now, when he drives along that particular section of road, in whatever direction, he can remember the feeling of anxiety that he was not where he should be. Somehow he was always letting somebody down. As parents, wanting to do the very best we can for our family, the intensity of such feelings is not to be under-estimated, and such emotion can sometimes threaten to crush us completely.

Guilt is not only a hard emotion to live with; it can also be an incredibly powerful motivating force in our lives. We feel guilty that we have not prevented our child's illness, so we don't correct them when they need to be corrected. We feel guilty that we don't have the emotional reserves for our other children, so we shower them with expensive presents that we probably can't afford. The sense of guilt that we have as parents can drive us to feel as if we are somehow to blame for all the awful stuff that has happened to our family, and so we have to make it up to our children constantly. Speaking from personal experience, this is far too heavy a burden to bear. For one thing, how on earth can we make up for our family's suffering? What, or how much, do we have to do, or say, or give, that will be enough to cancel out the debt that we think we owe them? My guess is that we're never going to get to the point where we feel it's OK that our child, or our family, has suffered as they have. The truth of it is that it's not OK, and for us as parents it

57

never will be OK. Our children's suffering will always seem totally unacceptable: I know it does to me.

So what do we do? Well, I believe that we have to choose to believe that their suffering is not a debt we have to pay, or could ever hope to pay. In other words, it's not our fault. We have to stop blaming ourselves. We live in a world that is not as it should be. It's a world where heartaches and tragedies will come into our life and the lives of those we love. 'Here on earth,' Jesus says, 'you will have many trials and sorrows. But take heart, because I have overcome the world' (John 16:33). The sort of heartache that we go through, seeing the suffering of our children, is not something that we can just recover from. It's something that needs to be set right.

The Bible has a word for this: redemption. The Bible says that some day God is going to set things right completely—maybe not today, maybe not tomorrow, but the day will come. 'He will swallow up death forever. The Sovereign Lord will wipe away the tears from all faces' (Isaiah 25:8, NIV). Until that day, we need to stop trying to change circumstances that are out of our control. In other words, we need to stop trying to repay, out of our own sense of false guilt, a debt to our children that isn't ours to pay.

It's also true that sometimes not all of the guilt we carry is false. As parents, we have to accept that sometimes we will get things wrong, sometimes very wrong. We may have made lifestyle choices, for example, that have contributed to our child's condition, or not given the right priority to their needs. Deep down we know that this is the case, and we may find it hard to like ourselves as a result. We may have lost our patience or our temper with our children; we may have set inappropriate boundaries. We all make mistakes, but, speaking from personal experience, there is nothing that weighs so heavily on our heart as when our mistakes result in our children getting hurt. This sort of mistake often causes us to feel over-whelmed by a sense of guilt, and guilt can be a very heavy load to carry. In fact, we may find that we can't carry it and it threatens to crush us completely.

There is another way, however. There is an alternative to the burden of guilt, and that's the healing power of forgiveness. As parents, especially parents of a child with a life-threatening illness, one of the most important, yet difficult, choices we will ever need to make is the choice to forgive ourselves. It's hard to know why we find this so difficult, since if Jesus Christ gave his life for us, he isn't going to turn round and condemn us; but tragically, all too often, we choose to continue to condemn ourselves.

So now there is no condemnation for those who belong to Christ Jesus. For the power of the life-giving Spirit has freed you through Christ Jesus from the power of sin that leads to death.

ROMANS 8:1–2

Today, right now, God longs to pour the restoring power of his love and forgiveness into our lives. He longs to set us free from the shackles of guilt, but the sad truth is that while we hold ourselves in unforgiveness, he can't. We hold the key to our own prison cell: we are both prisoner and jailer.

Is anything stopping you today from turning the key that you have in your hand—through making a choice to forgive yourself—opening the door of your prison of guilt and allowing God to reach into your life and rescue you?

What a miserable person I am. Who will rescue me from this body that is doomed to die? Thank God! Jesus Christ will rescue me.

ROMANS 7:24–25 (CEV)

❖

Chapter 8

PREVENTING SIBLING RIVALRY

When Joseph's brothers saw that their father loved him more than any
of them, they hated him and could not speak a kind word to him.
GENESIS 37:4 (NIV)

So far, we have focused a great deal on the specific needs of the child
who is ill, and it's right and proper that we do, because we have to
understand those needs. As is the case with my family, however,
many of us have more than one child, and this presents us with
a unique set of challenges. Somehow we also have to hear and
understand the needs of our other children: they need us too!

This may sound obvious, especially if you have never had any
personal experience of parenting under such circumstances, and of
course in many ways it is obvious, but it's also easier said than done.
There were times when I came home after spending day after day
in hospital with my son, and felt as if I had nothing left to give to
anyone, not even my daughters. At those times, although I loved
them dearly, I was too exhausted to play a game with them or give
them my full, undivided attention, which they both needed and
deserved. I felt like Peter, of whom Jesus said, 'Though the spirit is
willing enough, the body is weak!' (Matthew 26:41). I just needed
to sleep. Often, it seems, the siblings of the sick child can get rather
short-changed when it comes to our attention and time, and it's
hard on them in all kinds of ways. Imagine how it must feel from
their perspective. Let's put ourselves in their shoes for a moment.

Your brother or sister is getting all the time, attention and
presents—and this may be not just Mummy's or Daddy's time
and attention, but Grandma's and Grandpa's, aunts' and uncles'
and even schoolteachers'. During stays in hospital, either Mummy

or Daddy is hardly ever at home with you, and you miss them very much. You miss being tucked in by them, or having them read your bedtime story, because it's only they who know how to do the funny voices, and only they who know how to make you feel warm and safe inside. Sometimes, when they do come home, they're tired and irritable, and you begin to wonder what you've done wrong to upset them. Maybe they don't love you so much any more. They don't seem to want to play the games they used to play with you, like football in the garden, or bake cakes in the kitchen. They just want to sit down. Sometimes they look sad, and sometimes they even start crying. (Maybe your child has never seen you cry before. Have you thought about the effect that has?) You're not really sure what it's about, except that something must have happened with your sick brother or sister again.

The grown-ups start to have whispered conversations with each other, and use strange words like 'chemotherapy', or talk about strange things like 'cell counts', and that sounds scary. You don't know what it all means, except that it involves more doctors coming into your house and more times when Mummy or Daddy will be away at the hospital.

You don't like to see your brother or sister in pain, but sometimes you feel jealous and wish it was you who was ill instead of them, because then you would be the one getting all the fuss and attention. Sometimes it doesn't seem fair that they can get away with things that you can't. They can be really naughty and not get told off, and then when you're naughty, Mummy or Daddy shouts at you twice as loudly as they ever did before. Sometimes you feel angry towards your brother or sister, and may even feel like hurting them. Then you feel bad, because you know that's not a kind thing to do. You may begin to think that you must just be a bad person, but you promise yourself that you must never tell anyone that.

I could go on, but the point is that these are just some of the many emotions and lifestyle changes with which other children in the family may have to cope. It's very hard on them, and, difficult though it is for us as parents, we must recognize and acknowledge how much the siblings of the ill child suffer. If we don't pay attention to their needs, they will try to find less constructive ways of making us pay attention. Attention-seeking can be manifested in all sorts of ways, through bad behaviour (such as uncontrollable outbursts of temper, hitting or biting other children or adults, becoming verbally abusive), showing an increasing resentment of the ill brother or sister, refusing to do school work, feigning illness themselves, or becoming withdrawn. These types of behaviour pattern are really the child screaming out, 'Listen to me! I'm hurting and confused too!'

As parents, we need to find a way to focus on our children's legitimate need for attention. The temptation is, of course, just to focus on the presenting 'bad' behaviour, but we need to remember that behaviour comes out of belief. It's the belief that gives life to the behaviour, not the other way round. Often, as a result of such family trauma, these children have damaged beliefs about themselves and life.

Be careful what you think because your thoughts run your life.
PROVERBS 4:23 (NEW CENTURY VERSION)

In the face of the apparently conflicting needs of our ill child and our other children, it's easy to feel completely overwhelmed and out of our depth. Sometimes it seems as if we can't do right without doing wrong, as if whatever choice we make will involve letting down someone we love. Before we go too far along the path of self-condemnation, however, we need to acknowledge the uniquely challenging and draining situation that we find ourselves in. We need to appreciate the fact that we simply cannot cut ourselves in two (or three, as in my situation) for our different children. Sometimes we have to make a choice about where, and with whom, we spend our time and energy; and sometimes we are going to get it wrong, get things out of balance. I can think of many occasions when (with that amazing gift of hindsight) I can see that I made wrong choices.

The key thing to remember, in addressing or preventing damaging beliefs in our children, is that there is a choice to be made. All our children need us. So often though, in my experience, we can become absorbed with the needs of our ill child (especially in crisis times) to the extent that we can't see anything else going on around us. We miss our other children's cries for help. This is understandable, of course, but if we are to build a secure and happy family over the long term, somehow we have to try to keep focused on the needs of our whole family.

We also have to try to encourage other close family members and friends to do the same. Grandparents may need to be told to buy presents and arrange special treats for all the grandchildren, not just the one who is ill. After all, as we have seen, each of the children is suffering in different ways.

It's not always easy to explain to other people the need to give as much time, attention and special treats to our other children. I remember that when David was first diagnosed with cancer, I was approached by a charity that wanted to pay for him to go to Disneyland in Florida for two weeks. The deal was that he went away with only trained medical staff to care for him. As a mother, this presented me with two dilemmas. It was a very moving thought that people had actually given a great deal of time and effort to raise the necessary funds for him to go. My first dilemma, though, was that my son was only seven years old. Even if he had been well, I wouldn't have wanted him to go away for two weeks with people that I didn't know; and I'm quite sure, knowing my son, that he wouldn't have wanted to go either. My other dilemma was this: what message would it send to my two daughters, who weren't invited? How would they feel when, once again, all the attention was on their brother? How would they feel when he came home sharing stories about places and experiences that they could only dream of?

I don't wish to appear ungrateful to those who made the very generous offer, or to suggest that this sort of thing is wrong for every family, but James and I certainly felt that it would not be helpful for ours. As it turned out, we were approached by another organization that arranged trips for children who were seriously or terminally ill, which included the whole family. So the five of us had the most fantastic three-day trip to Disneyland in Paris, giving us all some very happy shared memories.

Of course, it's by no means a lack of care that motivates people to focus only on the ill child. It's just that his or her needs tend to be far more obvious and tangible. For example, my son had no hair for long periods of time, and as soon as people saw him, they could understand something of the hardship he was going through. They could appreciate that he might be scared, and that he had certainly suffered, so he needed some extra support and encouragement. On the other hand, my two daughters' fear, suffering and need for comfort were not so obvious—and while they were not so easy to spot, they were just as real.

As parents of a child with a life-threatening illness, we face a unique set of challenges in building a family, and one of the most difficult of those challenges is ensuring that all our children feel equally loved, valued and cared for. All our children need to have their legitimate needs met for unconditional love, reassurance and relaxed fun times with us. We also have to accept, however, that sometimes we're going to get things out of balance, and we must not be too hard on ourselves when this happens, because it's fairly inevitable that it will happen. As parents, we have not only our own pain to process, but many other conflicting emotional demands placed on us as well.

The crucial thing, though, is that we try. We try to understand what all our children are going through. The importance of this is not to be underestimated if we are to succeed in building strong parent-to-sibling and sibling-to-sibling ties. One of the most tragic consequences of a child's life-threatening illness is when another child in the family no longer sees a brother or sister, but a rival who threatens their position in their parents' hearts.

❖

Chapter 9

THE NECESSITY FOR REST

Come to me, all you who are weary and burdened, and I will give you rest.
MATTHEW 11:28 (NIV)

Living day after day, week after week, year after year, with the stress that parenting brings in the face of the life-threatening illness of our child can be exhausting. This isn't surprising, since there are so many physical, emotional and spiritual demands placed on us as parents. I had times when I was so tired that I felt somehow disconnected from my surroundings. Other people's voices seemed to fade in and out, and I wasn't able to remember normal everyday words. 'You need to get some sleep,' people would say to me, and of course they were right. We all know how refreshing a good night's sleep is, and how important it is to our sense of well-being.

Getting that sleep, however, isn't always as easy as it might seem. Not only might there be the practical problem of being unable to leave our sick child's bedside, but we can also face emotional barriers to getting our rest. I can remember falling on to my bed sometimes, without even the energy to get into it properly, and shutting my eyes, expecting to be 'out like a light', only to find that two or three hours later, when it was time to get up again, either I hadn't slept a wink or my sleep had been fitful.

The problem was that as soon as I lay down, my mind would start whirling. I would think of all that had happened during the day, and as my mind started wandering, I would think of what might lie ahead. The hours spent awake and alone with my thoughts in the middle of the night were some of the scariest times I have ever experienced. I used to imagine the worst-case scenarios, and before

I knew it, in my mind they had become reality, leaving me in a state of blind panic. I understood in a new way what the phrase 'terrors of the night' meant.

I have spoken to other parents in a similar position and found that many of them have had similar experiences. We end up running away from quiet times on our own, or times doing nothing but 'resting'. Somehow it feels safer to keep busy, keep ourselves occupied, rather than risk standing still and being ambushed by the fears and uncertainties brought by our wandering thoughts. Of course, such avoidance of our God-given need for rest can be very damaging.

God wants his loved ones to get their proper rest.
PSALM 127:2 (LB)

Physically, we may begin to feel run down and vulnerable to viruses and infections. My dentist always knew when I was going through particularly stressful times, because the result was an abscess on one of my teeth. Emotionally, without adequate rest we have a limited ability to cope, and can easily lose perspective. Even the smallest things, like breaking a mug, or the traffic lights turning red, can reduce us to tears. I must have had many strange looks in the past when I was driving! Spiritually, we may feel that our 'well has run dry' and that within us is nothing except the most terrible sense of emptiness. It can feel as if we have a hole at the core of our being that drains us of any sense of life.

What do we do? How do we find the physical and emotional space that we need to get our proper rest? Some people may choose medication as a means of stopping the mind from whirling, to help them get some sleep. I think this is a perfectly valid choice, and I am certainly not against such medication: I've used it myself. I also think that, on its own, it is not enough to give the sort of restoration and peace to the body, soul and spirit that we desperately need.

Speaking from personal experience, it's only the peace of God that can and does provide the total rest and refreshment that we crave.

Those who live in the shelter of the Most High
will find rest in the shadow of the Almighty.
This I declare of the Lord:
He alone is my refuge, my place of safety;
he is my God, and I am trusting him.
For he will rescue you from every trap
and protect you from the fatal plague.
He will shield you with his wings.
He will shelter you with his feathers.
His faithful promises are your armour and protection.
Do not be afraid of the terrors of the night,
nor fear the dangers of the day,
nor dread the plague that stalks in darkness,
nor the disaster that strikes at midday.
PSALM 91:1–6

Many years ago, a painting competition took place in which the subject was 'Peace'. There were two prize winners. One had gone to the English Lake District and painted a beautiful picture of a warm summer's day, with a lake in the foreground and a mountain range in the background. There was a tranquillity to the scene, and it was the kind of picture that made you want to be there—even more so, in my opinion, if they had painted an ice-cream van in the corner!

Anyway, the other artist had gone to the south-western corner of England and painted a storm on the Cornish coast. About a third of the way across the picture, a high cliff descended into the rough sea, where huge waves lashed the bottom of the cliff and sent their white surf high into the air. The skies were heavy with black clouds, the rain was beating down, and a tree on the top of the cliff was pushed to a 45-degree angle as the winds blew in from the Atlantic. The picture made you feel cold, and glad to be indoors. Halfway up the cliff was a cleft in the rock. In the cleft was a nest and on the nest was a gull, sitting with its eyes closed. The artist called his picture 'Peace' and won first prize.

The point is this: we have to come to terms with the fact that we're probably never going to experience the sort of peace that we can find for ourselves in our own understanding, the sort of peace that comes through everything around us being right. That's the sort of peace highlighted by the first painting, of a warm summer's day. The particular nature of the trauma we have experienced, and continue to experience, means that our lives aren't those 'blue skies' sort of lives. Our child's illness has meant that our days contain dark clouds, and sometimes howling gales. Our peace, therefore, has to be like the peace found in the second painting— the peace of that gull on the nest, sheltered and secure in the cleft in the rock.

I must admit that I have been slow to discover the sort of rest and peace that God can give 'whatever the circumstances' (Philippians 4:11, NIV). I have spent many hours praying that God would change my external circumstances, praying that I would wake up and find that everything was back to how it used to be before my son was ill. 'If only I could see blue skies,' I'd think, 'then, and only then, will I really be able to feel at peace.' Of course, there's nothing wrong with asking God to take hard things away from us. Jesus himself asked as much in the garden of Gethsemane. 'My Father!' he prayed, 'If it is possible, let this cup of suffering be taken away from me' (Matthew 26:39). There are times, of course, when God does take things away from us, when miraculous physical healings do happen, but there are so many other times when this doesn't seem to be the case—when we, like Jesus, are called to walk the way of the cross—and it hurts. Perhaps one of the greatest miracles of all, however, is that when we are called to carry on in the face of storms and driving rain, when everything around us makes no sense to us, God offers us a peace that transcends it all, peace and rest that really does transcend our understanding. This peace is not dependent upon external circumstances, but on the internal reality of the security that is ours as Christians in Christ Jesus.

I can remember many times, throughout my son's illness, when I felt so anxious that there seemed to be a crushing weight on my chest, and I even found it difficult to breathe. I discovered that trying to find any sense of peace and rest in my own strength, through my own understanding, was impossible in those times. It was only when I started to pray or listen to worship tapes that I began to feel a lightening of the burden, that I could start to breathe again. Through those experiences, more than anything else I have ever been through, I have learnt how wonderful it is to 'rest in the shadow of the Almighty' (Psalm 91:1) and feel a sense of being restored in body, soul and spirit.

I know it, I have experienced it, and yet I also know that I don't 'go there' as often as I should. I just pop in and out of that nest on the rock face as if it's some kind of 'holiday inn', whereas the truth is that that shelter should be our permanent residence. When we become Christians, it means that we are 'in Christ': we are securely hidden in that rock. We 'abide' in him. Too many times, I give in to anxious thoughts, trying to work them out in my own strength and my own understanding, and I find that the rest and peace I so desperately need elude me.

Don't be impressed with your own wisdom. Instead, fear the Lord and turn your back on evil. Then you will gain renewed health and vitality.
PROVERBS 3:7–8

At some point, storm clouds will gather in the life of anyone who walks through this troubled world. Life is fragile for even the best, cleverest and strongest of us. The good news—no, the great news— is that we have a heavenly Father who longs to give us all the resources we need to cope, who longs to give us the rest and peace we crave. The question is whether we will let him do it. Will we choose to shelter under the shadow of his wings?

I call as my heart grows faint;
lead me to the rock that is higher than I.
For you have been my refuge,
a strong tower against the foe.
I long to dwell in your tent forever
and take refuge in the shelter of your wings.
PSALM 61:2–4 (NIV)

❖

Chapter 10

BOUNDARIES AND BATTLES

My child, don't ignore it when the Lord disciplines you, and don't be discouraged when he corrects you. For the Lord corrects those he loves, just as a father corrects a child in whom he delights.
PROVERBS 3:11–12

Most of us, as parents, know the value of good boundaries in the family. Boundaries set limits. They say to the child, 'You can go this far and no further', and they bring a sense of security, stability and self-worth. Our children know that if they overstep the boundary, there will be consequences, and they will be punished. Of course, the vast majority of us punish our children not because we enjoy inflicting pain, but because we're concerned for our children's development. We know that, in order to become morally strong and good, our children must learn the difference between right and wrong, and that's why we seek to establish and enforce boundaries in their lives.

It's somewhat ironic, therefore, that although the existence of appropriate boundaries helps to keep our children safe and secure, when our children are first diagnosed with a life-threatening illness we may feel an overwhelming desire to remove all such boundaries. At the time when our children need security the most, we take away the very mechanism that gives it to them. Why do we do this when, logically, it doesn't make any sense? Well, speaking as a mother who at first did unwisely remove most of the boundaries surrounding her son, it wasn't a decision made from logic: it was a highly emotional one. I felt powerless to change anything. I couldn't take away my son's cancer; nor could I prevent him from going through harrowing medical treatment. It was agonizing to see my son suffering as he did, and to feel that I had absolutely no control over it. Out of a desire to make myself feel better, just as much as to cheer him up, I would give, do or say anything to make him feel even a tiny bit happier.

I think James began to dread leaving me alone with David. He would come back after a couple of hours and find that I had promised David all sorts of things that we could not afford, and that under normal circumstances we would never have dreamed of giving him. A day left completely on my own with him would probably have meant taking out a second mortgage on our home! I remember that on one occasion, when my son was coming round from a general anaesthetic, I ended up promising him an 'Ice Planet' Lego set (at the time, very expensive and top-of-the-range), a trip to a computer game shop about 100 miles from where we lived, and a super-size McDonald's for his tea. All this was promised in the space of about half an hour.

Of course, for a few brief moments the thought of those presents and special treats did make things a bit better for my son. Sometimes when I'd promised him something, I'd get a little flicker of a smile, and in those seconds, whatever the treat was, or however much it cost, it seemed worth it. The trouble was, though, that had I continued much longer, I would have stored up tremendous problems elsewhere. It would have been difficult for our girls not to have felt increasingly left out or jealous of all the special treats their brother had been given, thereby sowing seeds of resentment towards him.

Do you like honey? Don't eat too much of it, or it will make you sick!
PROVERBS 25:16

It wasn't just boundaries on material possessions that I wanted to remove for David; it was also behavioural boundaries. Issues such as good manners didn't seem important when he was suffering so much. Making sure he still said 'please' and 'thank you' seemed irrelevant. What did it matter, for example, if he was rude to the nurse? Did it really matter in the grand scheme of things? Well, actually, yes, it did matter. It mattered because, as parents, our role is to develop well-rounded children, but it also mattered for David's sense of security. He needed to know that, no matter how hard he pushed against it, the same boundary line was still going to be there. He needed to know that in the midst of the uncertain and confusing environment he now occupied, some things stayed the same.

This was brought home to me one very painful but emotionally healing day. I had been at David's bedside for hours, although he had not wanted to communicate with me. James arrived at the hospital and suggested that I took a break. As I said goodbye to David, he just shrugged his shoulders at me. I had never before seen my son so disrespectful towards me. My husband immediately told David to apologize for his behaviour. I was pleading with James, behind David's, back to let it go, not to make a fuss. But wisely (I say that now), James wouldn't. At the time, I just couldn't bear to see my son being told off. Again and again David refused to say he was sorry, and the confrontation continued, with me in tears. My husband was not going to back down, though, and he pointed out to David that he might have lost his kidney, but the doctors hadn't removed his manners as well. Eventually, David conceded and murmured an apology.

I remember going from the ward and absolutely howling my eyes out, and I remember my husband following me, also in tears. There were tears all round, that day, but it was also a major turning point for the three of us. David had tested the boundary to the limit, but found that his father had kept it intact. It hadn't crumbled beneath him, and this actually proved to be the source of a great deal of comfort to David. After that time, for example, David would take his medication only from his father, and wanted him there at every major trauma. Why? Because he felt safe and secure. That turned out to be a very important battle for us, as parents, to have won.

There are some battles, though, that in the grand scheme of things aren't so important. They don't really matter, and one of the areas needing the most wisdom is knowing which do and which don't matter. What battles should we fight and what should we let go? Even under normal circumstances, we can't, and indeed shouldn't, fight them all. The way our children dress, for example, especially as they get older, is not our battle to fight. Our children need a certain freedom to express their own opinions, which, like it or not, may well be different from ours. In fact, since they are not us, it's very healthy that they do have different likes and dislikes. Children need a certain amount of freedom of thought and action in order to begin to define who they are. Choosing our battles carefully is not easy. We can go to war with our children over things that aren't going to make any significant difference, and meanwhile we let other boundaries crumble when we should have kept them strongly and firmly in place.

When we have a child with a life-threatening illness, knowing what battles are important is even more difficult and potentially painful to determine. One reason is that children in this situation will often want to go to war over *something*. It may not mean that they are being deliberately disobedient, rather that they are trying to find something they can control in a world that suddenly seems very out of control, in a world where they feel powerless. Almost at the start of David's illness, he decided that he wasn't going to take any medication—a decision that didn't make any sense to me and my husband. He even stopped eating bananas, which he loved, when a doctor told him to eat them because he needed the potassium they contained, and he would rather be in pain, or sick, than take his medication.

This caused both my husband and me an incredible amount of stress. We coaxed him to take his anti-sickness medication, cajoled him, got cross with him, tried all sorts of tempting ways to disguise the taste, and even tried holding him still while one of us poured it down his throat, but he was having none of it. If you have ever tried to get a child to take any medication that they didn't want, you will appreciate how difficult this was. Whole bottles got spilt or spat out. In our efforts to get him to swallow, tears were shed. In fact, an altogether miserable and distressing time was had by all, until one day I had a conversation with Sue, the hospital play specialist I mentioned earlier. She managed to shed some new light on the situation, making it easier for me to understand why David was making the seemingly irrational choice not to take his medication.

The bottom line was that he was doing it precisely because it was something he could make a choice over. I began to appreciate how, in the course of his illness, so many choices had been taken away from him. He had to sleep in a hospital bed; had to put up with doctors prodding and poking him; had to have operations and so on. None of these things he could do anything about. He could, however, choose not to open his mouth for any oral medication. If he decided he wasn't going to swallow, no one could make him. Fortunately for us all, David's oral medication (he had his chemotherapy and antibiotics intravenously) was prescribed to ease his discomfort rather than treat his condition—painkillers, for example, or anti-sickness medication.

David's decision to fight this particular battle was not so much about being disobedient as about his need to make choices, to have options. As my husband and I began to understand this, we decided that we did not have to fight the battle. (Of course, if his chemotherapy had been taken orally, it would have been a different story.) So we decided to present the alternatives to David and let him make the choice himself. We told him that he could either be sick and in pain, or take his medication, but the decision was entirely his. We expected that, having empowered him in such a way, having given him back the choice, he would be sensible and choose to take his medication, but he didn't. We then had to respect his choice and watch him suffer unnecessarily, which was incredibly frustrating for us as parents. David, however, seemed to think it was worth paying the sacrifice of physical comfort to gain some emotional well-being—to make the statement that he did have some control and choice, that his opinions were going to be noticed.

It's very difficult, as parents of a child with a life-threatening illness, who live in a world of such uncertainty, to know what boundaries need to remain firm so that our children feel secure. As we have seen already, we need wisdom to know what battles we do need to fight, and on what occasions we have to respect our children's need for choice and freedom of expression. This can be made even more difficult by the nature of the illness our child faces. We may not like to admit it, but there can be a sense in which not knowing whether, or for how long, our child may live makes us less motivated to give thought to the future. The issues of boundaries and battles seem unimportant. We can begin to wonder what point there is in encouraging them in their education if they may never need it. Why teach them the value of money if they're never going to have to manage a household budget? Although understandable, these sorts of attitude can't bring 'life in all its fullness' (John 10:10) to our children. Why? Because they don't give our children the opportunity to be all they could be for however long they may have on this earth.

The truth is that only God knows all the days allotted to our children. Meanwhile, for us as parents, our role, privilege and joy is to be partners with God in developing children of character, children who, despite any physical difficulties they may have, reflect the personality and passion that God has given to them.

Discipline your son, and he will give you peace; he will bring delight to your soul.
PROVERBS 29:17 (NIV)

❖

Chapter 11

LETTING GO

There is a time for everything,
a season for every activity under heaven.
A time to be born and a time to die.
A time to plant and a time to harvest.
A time to kill and a time to heal.
A time to tear down and a time to rebuild.
A time to cry and a time to laugh.
A time to grieve and a time to dance.
A time to scatter stones and a time to gather stones.
A time to embrace and a time to turn away.
A time to search and a time to lose.
A time to keep and a time to throw away.
A time to tear and a time to mend.
A time to be quiet and a time to speak up.
A time to love and a time to hate.
A time for war and a time for peace.
ECCLESIASTES 3:1–8

One of our main roles as parents is to love our children towards adulthood and independence. Even under normal circumstances, this produces many challenges. How do we know the right level of responsibility to give to our children at the right time? How do we let them have enough freedom to make their own mistakes, and not allow ourselves to rescue them before they've had the opportunity to learn from those mistakes? What social skills will our children need, to teach them to value other people and yet not allow themselves to be walked over by others? How do we communicate the dangers of life without crushing their adventurous spirits? How do we get to know the necessary information about what is going on in their lives, and yet respect their right to privacy?

These are just some of the potential minefields that parents have to negotiate in the course of developing a right independence in children. They all seem dangerous to me, but the truth is that if we don't seek to address these issues and other issues like them, other dangers lurk in the wings. Our children may become rebellious, for example, as they find illegitimate ways of satisfying a legitimate need for independence, or they may fail to find their own sense of identity, to be separate from us. If we are to produce confident children with healthy levels of self-esteem, who know the purpose for which they were made, we have to learn to let them go. This isn't emotionally easy for any parent, but for parents of a child with a life-threatening illness, it can be many, many times more difficult.

Many parents in this position, myself included, have a very understandable desire to overprotect their children. We want to wrap them in cotton-wool, and the desire to protect them can get completely out of perspective. There are many reasons for this. We may feel that since we don't know how long we will have them, we want them all to ourselves for every possible moment. We may feel that since we can't protect them from their actual condition, we need to make up for it by protecting them from everything else in that big bad world out there. We may become so used to having to protect them because of their physical condition that to expose them to other people, or other situations, is too much of a risk. Sometimes, this is true, of course. During my son's chemotherapy treatment, there were periods of time when he had absolutely no white cells in his body. The white cells are the blood cells that help us fight infection, and in the times when he had none at all, it was very necessary to limit his contact with people and environments prone to germs, such as public meeting places.

The problem comes when, as parents, we get used to feeling that we have to shield our children from all aspects of life. I know from my own experience that when David's white cell count recovered, I still found it difficult to let go and allow him to venture into the world again. Emotionally, it just seemed too risky, even though, logically, I knew that the physical risk was greatly reduced. Of course, life itself is a risk, and if we don't allow our children to take calculated risks, we will produce children who are afraid to embrace life. They will be for ever in a cocoon-like state, wrapped in a shell of anxiety, never breaking out to become a butterfly and reaching the heights that God always intended them to reach.

For God did not give us a spirit of timidity, but a spirit of power, of love and of self-discipline.
2 TIMOTHY 1:7 (NIV)

Throughout my son's illness I had, at times, an overwhelming desire to keep him quite literally in that cocoon-like state. I wanted to keep him wrapped up in his quilt on our sofa at home, where I could be sure he was safe and not exposed to any risks whatsoever—except falling off the sofa! I was, and still am, extremely prone to trying to overprotect my son. James and I are in the process of planning our first trip away, leaving David on his own for the first time. Although he is nearly 18, very trustworthy and sensible, it has been really difficult to make the break. I have asked him so many times whether he's sure he's going to be all right staying on his own that it's become embarrassing for both of us.

It isn't only towards my son that I have been somewhat over-protective. My two daughters have also had to endure their fair share of 'Are you sure you'll be all right?' questions too. When serious, life-threatening illness strikes one of our children, we lose our assumption that this sort of thing doesn't happen to our family. The unwritten law that previously ruled our mind—that we will die before our children—gets rubbed out, and we become all too aware of the apparent randomness of suffering. Once that happens, if we are not careful, the floodgates are opened to the thought, 'If this can happen, then why not anything else?'

When we begin to allow this chain of thought to dominate our mind, the world becomes an extremely scary place. We become governed by 'What if...?' What if my child learns to drive a car, and then has a crash? Perhaps it's better that they never learn to drive at all. What if they go in the car of a friend who isn't as sensible as they are, and they crash? Perhaps it would be better that they *did* learn to drive. Better still, their father should take them everywhere, at least until they're safely drawing their pension.

What if my husband and I go away for the weekend, leave our children to manage on their own, and one of them gets meningitis? They won't know what it is, and if it remains undiagnosed because I'm not there, well, we all know where that could lead. What if one of them has an allergic reaction to a bee sting? After all, how can I be sure that they're not allergic to bee stings? They've never been stung by a bee before. So what if they did get stung, and I was in the house instead of the garden, so I didn't see them fall into unconsciousness? Didn't I read in a magazine about that happening to someone? It can happen—and if it can happen, then why shouldn't it happen to my family? If one of my children can have cancer, then surely they can be stung by a bee!

This may seem to you like the ramblings of some tortured individual, and maybe you're right! The truth is, though, that I have had many such thoughts since my son's diagnosis. My previously held optimistic view of life and all its opportunities has been for ever coloured by my son's illness, and consequently, life now holds many more potential dangers in my mind.

We cannot live by 'What if...?', however, which is one reason why Jesus said, 'Therefore do not worry about tomorrow, for tomorrow will worry about itself. Each day has enough trouble of its own' (Matthew 6:34, NIV). Nor can we project all those 'what ifs' on to our children. We want our children to embrace life, not to be held back by fear and anxiety. We want our children to learn to fly, which means that they will need to stretch their wings and one day leave the nest. For those of us who have a child with a life-threatening illness, the temptation is to restrict their movements because of our own pain and damage—to hem them in.

Letting our children go under such circumstances requires a great deal of wisdom. Each child must be given the right amount of freedom, appropriate to their unique circumstances. My son spent a whole year absent from school at one period during his illness. His educational development didn't suffer at all (in fact, he was ahead of his class in maths), since he had a fantastic home tutor, who is also a close family friend and was sensitive to all of David's needs. I am quite sure, however, that his emotional development was affected. In many ways, the life experiences that David had gone through belied his age. In some respects, David experienced more in his first ten years than many of us do in a lifetime. He knew words, and concepts such as the function of platelets in his blood and the consequences of not having enough of them, or the purpose of magnetic resonance imaging scanners, which ideally should never be part of a child's vocabulary or understanding. In those ways he was wise beyond his years. At the same time, other parts of his emotional development were stunted. The lack of a school environment for such an extended period of time meant that he had very little time away from his family. This contributed to the fact that he was far less independent than our daughters were at a similar age. As a result, giving David the same sort of freedom that we gave our girls would have been scary for him, rather than freeing. We must treat our children as unique individuals in all circumstances, but perhaps even more so when they have been through the unique life experiences that serious illness brings.

There is another way in which parents of a child with a life-threatening illness struggle with letting go: they can let go too soon and withdraw too much of their emotional and physical support. Some parents choose to spend a very limited time with their sick child, while others take on a professional carer's role. They disconnect emotionally from the parent–child relationship. Under the circumstances, it may sound very strange—harsh, even—for parents to do that, but such emotional withdrawal often comes from the parent's own pain and damage, manifesting itself in a different way from the overprotective parent's. The underprotective parent who tries to let go and push their child towards independence too quickly is often really saying, 'I think you're going to die, so I'm going to try to stop loving you as much, so that it won't hurt so deeply when I do lose you. I'm going to start my grieving now.'

Observing this approach can be quite distressing. I myself have seen parents who just seemed to abandon their children emotionally, and it is hard to witness. At meal-times in hospital, my husband and I fed other children on my son's ward because their parents were once again absent. Very often, however, it's not because the parents don't care. In fact, ironically, it scares them how much they do care. They are so scared of facing the pain of loss that they put up a wall round their heart, and their emotional withdrawal can be a coping mechanism—a form of self-protection.

Because it is often difficult to empathize with such parents, it's very easy to judge them. I can remember feeling really angry towards one parent on my son's hospital ward, who, in my opinion, let go of most of her parental responsibilities. Her daughter had leukaemia, and she was often left on her own while her mother had her hair done or went clothes shopping. The child's grandparents, and not her mother, were present at the majority of the medical procedures that the little girl needed. As a mother, I found this really upsetting and mistook her physical absence for an absence of love for her child. After many conversations with her grandparents, however, a picture began to emerge of a mother who was just as scared as I was, but who was running away. She didn't have the emotional resources to stand and face the reality of the situation: she was running scared. I now feel a great deal of sympathy for those who cope by emotionally withdrawing (particularly when children are involved), as they are often greatly misunderstood. The amazing thing to remember, though, is that God knows. God sees past everyone else's judgments and even past someone's own misguided beliefs. God sees us and sees straight to the heart of all our fears and anxieties.

The Lord does not look at the things man looks at. Man looks at the outward appearance, but the Lord looks at the heart.
1 SAMUEL 16:7 (NIV)

Only God knows whether or not our children will reach adulthood, but let's not confuse age with maturity, as they need not necessarily be the same thing. Our joy and privilege in parenting is to develop emotionally whole and mature individuals. Our child's physical condition may never be healed or corrected, but they are more than just physical matter. They also have a spirit and a soul, which need not be held back or impaired by their physical condition. God has plans and purposes for our children that are not solely defined by their bodies. Our responsibility as parents, through appropriate letting go of our children, is to encourage the sort of growth and development that enable them to achieve their full potential in Christ. In other words, we should have as much respect for all that our children are, and all they can be, as their heavenly Father has for them.

You made all the delicate, inner parts of my body
and knit me together in my mother's womb.
Thank you for making me so wonderfully complex!
Your workmanship is marvellous—and how well I know it.
You watched me as I was being formed in utter seclusion,
as I was woven together in the dark of the womb.
You saw me before I was born.
Every day of my life was recorded in your book.
Every moment was laid out
before a single day had passed.
How precious are your thoughts about me, O God!
They are innumerable!

I can't even count them;
they outnumber the grains of sand!
PSALM 139:13–18

Letting go and encouraging independence in our children isn't easy for most parents, but it can be especially difficult for those of us whose world has been shaken by our child's life-threatening illness. Many of us in this situation have had to put our lives on hold in all kinds of ways. We may have had to give up careers and outside interests to be full-time carers for our child. As a result, our whole identity may have become defined by our child's illness. When this happens, it makes letting go so much more difficult. Although we may acknowledge in our heads that, despite their illness, it is good to encourage rightful, appropriate independence, our hearts may tell us something else. We may find that, without even realizing what's happened, we've become emotionally dependent on our child. We may find that our child's illness has meant that the 'apron strings' have become very entangled and our relationship with our child is far more complicated than we realized. Sometimes, letting our children go, encouraging them on to maturity, is as much about our having the courage to embrace life again as individuals in our own right.

So take a new grip with your tired hands and stand firm on
your shaky legs. Mark out a straight path for your feet. Then
those who follow you, though they are weak and lame, will
not stumble and fall but will become strong.
HEBREWS 12:12–13

84

❖

Chapter 12

BUILDING FOR TOMORROW

Therefore we do not lose heart. Though outwardly we are wasting away, yet inwardly we are being renewed day by day. For our light and momentary troubles are achieving for us an eternal glory that far outweighs them all. So we fix our eyes not on what is seen, but what is unseen. For what is seen is temporary, but what is unseen is eternal.
2 CORINTHIANS 4:16–18 (NIV)

One of the most frequent pieces of advice concerning David's illness that James and I have received has been to 'live for the day'. 'Make the most of every moment,' people say, and of course in many ways that's good, sound advice. One really positive thing that has come out of David's illness is that we have valued, and do value, our special times together. We certainly don't take them for granted in the way we would have done had we not had to live with an on-going threat to the life of one of our children. Birthdays, special family times and holidays become extra-significant when we are confronted with the very real possibility that this may be the last one we share together. And of course, there is a sense of great joy to be had from such precious moments.

Many times, however, it can be a bittersweet joy, because there is also a great deal of pain attached to the realization that this may be the last opportunity we have to enjoy a specific event or activity with our child. The people who say, 'Just make the most of every moment' don't always realize that it is not as simple as it sounds. Sometimes, making the most of every moment involves both joy and heart-rending pain. It was also difficult for me to find environments where, as a mother, I could express that pain. Other people couldn't always cope with hearing our fears, and when we said things like, 'I am so scared that this will be my son's last birthday', they often responded with, 'Don't be silly; you can't think like that.' The problem was that the thought was anything but silly. In fact, it was a very real possibility, and I did think like that sometimes.

I remember one bonfire night after David had relapsed with cancer. He was awaiting a major operation that would give us an idea of how far the cancer had spread, and whether treatment was to be continued. Anyway, in the spirit of 'living for the moment', we held a rather impromptu bonfire party. We had some fireworks at home for the children, cooked some special food, and enjoyed a great family time together. About halfway through the evening, however, the thought suddenly occurred to me that this could be the last bonfire night we had together as a family. This could be the last time David saw fireworks, or tasted toffee apples, or danced with sparklers. This might be the last time that my three children did these things together, and the emotion of such thoughts was so overwhelming that I simply couldn't contain it, and had to make some excuse about needing to go inside for a few moments. Once safely out of sight of the children, I just broke down and sobbed.

At such times, I was reminded of the words of the old hymn describing Jesus' crucifixion, 'Did e'er such love and sorrow meet?' That, for me, describes how I have often felt as I've travelled through the landmarks of 'normal' family life under the dark cloud of the life-threatening illness of our child. On the one hand, David's illness has taught me so much about valuing what I have and not taking things for granted, and as a result I have experienced many joyous and happy times with my family, times when I thought my heart would burst with the love that I had for my children. At the same time, though, I would often feel that my heart was about to break with the pain of the threat of losing our son.

It's strange how looking through the lenses of living with a life-threatening illness often means that we see in extremes. We see the very bright and the very dark. We see the real preciousness of what we have and the real terror of losing it. We see such amazing joy and such heart-rending sorrow. We see life and death.

The extremity and intensity of such emotions can be draining to live with. In fact, at times it can leave us feeling exhausted. The problem with the sentiment of 'just living for today', seeking to make the 'most of every moment', means that we're always living in that heightened emotional state. This is one reason why so many long-distance relationships fail. The pressure to enjoy the times the couple do have together means that neither is being real with the other. They're afraid to spoil their limited time by having a row, or by having an 'off day', so problems and disagreements never get aired. Instead, they fester underground, only to surface at a later time and sour the relationship. Living under such a pressure to 'perform' is unsustainable long-term, because it's not normal to live that way. Life cannot always be lived at breakneck speed and on emotional highs. We all need down times.

For those of us who are parents of a child with a life-threatening illness, 'making the most of every moment' may be an acceptable way to live for several weeks, but to live this way month after month, year after year, is altogether a different matter. Apart from the exhaustion it brings, it's not conducive to developing a relaxed or 'real' family environment. It's stressful for everyone to feel that they can never have times when they can't be bothered, or are just feeling a bit low.

As Christians, choosing 'not to worry about tomorrow' doesn't mean that we have to live on a constant emotional high, or in denial, or in the belief that there won't be a tomorrow. In fact, in my experience, one of the most courageous things that we can do is to live as if there will be a tomorrow, because, whatever shape it takes, that day will come. In other words, we need to choose life again. In the midst of uncertainty, we need to live lives that build for the future.

I have set before you life and death, blessings and curses. Now choose life, so that you and your children may live.
DEUTERONOMY 30:19 (NIV)

If we, as parents, choose to live with an attitude that means we are afraid to look to tomorrow, we will never build a stable environment for family life. Why? Because it's an environment where hope dies and, God knows, we all need hope.

'For I know the plans I have for you,' declares the Lord, 'plans to prosper you and not to harm you, plans to give you hope and a future.'
JEREMIAH 29:11 (NIV)

Our children need the sense of security and stability that looking ahead brings (albeit with the flexible approach that we have to adopt as parents of a child with a life-threatening illness). They also need us to build 'family traditions' that stay the same, so that they can look back on them. Such shared memories bring a sense of identity and belonging to all our children, and give them a healthy model to draw on if they become parents themselves.

For parents of a child with a life-threatening illness, the future can seem absolutely terrifying. If you have ever read *A Christmas Carol* by Charles Dickens, you may remember that, in the story, the miser Scrooge is visited by three ghosts who show him glimpses of various stages of his life. The ghost of Christmas Past shows him what has gone before, the ghost of Christmas Present shows him how he is currently living his life, and the ghost of Christmas Future shows him what lies ahead if he continues to live as he is doing. After the visit of the first ghost, Scrooge resigns himself to the visits of the other two. Even though he expects them, he says something very interesting. He remarks that, although he is frightened by the thought of all the ghosts, it is the ghost of Christmas Future that terrifies him most. Many of us, as parents of a child with a life-threatening illness, can identify very much with that fictional character. The thought of our future, of all that lies ahead, can take on almost nightmarish qualities, so we try to stay rooted where we are. The reality is, though, that this is a bit like trying to stand still on an escalator. Like it or not, we're moving forward—forward into the unknown.

As Christians, the truth is that as we look to an unknown future on this earth and the scary things we may have to face, we're not alone. 'God has said, "Never will I leave you; never will I forsake you." So we can say with confidence, "The Lord is my helper; I will not be afraid. What can man do to me?"' (Hebrews 13:5–6, NIV). We have a God on whom we can rely, and who remains 'the same yesterday and today and for ever' (Hebrews 13:8, NIV)—a God who knows everything that lies ahead of us as we take the next courageous step forward on our journey.

You hem me in—behind and before;
you have laid your hand upon me.
Such knowledge is too wonderful for me,
too lofty for me to attain.
Where can I go from your Spirit?
Where can I go to flee from your presence?
If I go up to the heavens, you are there;
if I make my bed in the depths, you are there.
If I rise on the wings of the dawn,
if I settle on the far side of the sea,
even there your hand will guide me,
your right hand will hold me fast.
If I say, 'Surely the darkness will hide me
and the light become night around me,'
even the darkness will not be dark to you;
the night will shine like the day,
for darkness is as light to you.
PSALM 139:5–12 (NIV)

There's even better news, as well! Though there may be much about this world that is uncertain (perhaps, as parents, we know that more than most), and much that just doesn't seem to make any sense, Christians know that they can build for tomorrow—not just here, while they are on this earth, but for all eternity in heaven. One day every tear will be wiped away, every wrong put right, and we will be all we were always intended to be.

As I write, my son is approaching his 18th birthday, and as he makes that transition into adulthood he carries with him the potential for more anxious times ahead as a result of his childhood cancer. Apart from the risk of the cancer returning, the new trial drugs that David received during his treatment themselves held many potential long-term dangers. Owing to the pioneering nature of these drugs, little research is available concerning any long-term damage they may have done to David's internal organs and general health. David is therefore something of a guinea pig in regard to the apparent success rate of his particular courses of treatment, and I have to admit that this thought is more than a little disconcerting to me.

Who knows what lies ahead for my son, or for my family, and who knows what lies ahead for yours? None of us knows. The great news is that God does know, and the miracle is that whatever tomorrow brings for any of us, it's not the end of the story. As Christians, we stand merely at the beginning, and we can look forward with confidence. We can have, and need to keep, an eternal perspective. Why? Because the best is yet to come!

'Here on earth you will have many trials and sorrows. But take heart, because I have overcome the world.'
JOHN 16:33

❖

If the subject of this book has raised questions for you or you want to know more about the Christian faith write to Jan Burn at:

Kingfisher Church
Moor St
Tredworth
Gloucester
GL1 4NJ

E-mail: janburn@kingfisher.org.uk
Website: www.kingfisher.org.uk/imstillstanding

IN THE PALM OF GOD'S HAND

A diary of living against the odds

WENDY BRAY

'Sharing a diary like this is about more than baring your soul. It's like taking your clothes off in public in mid-January and asking passers-by to throw snowballs at you. Not something you would do unless you hoped an awful lot of good would come of it. But here I am, doing it… Whatever good might result is God's to reveal. I would hope that it will involve glory to him and comfort and encouragment to others, as well as providing the occasional laugh.'

This prayer diary testifies how personal faith can transform the hardest of times, and how God's love and mercy still break through, no matter how tough the situation. Rob Parsons writes in the introduction: 'This is a book about trust. Not the kind of trust that says, "I know that soon it will be all right agin", but rather the kind that trusts God—anyway—sometimes because there is just nowhere else to go.'

ISBN 1 84101 336 6   £6.99

Available from your local Christian bookshop or, in case of difficulty, using the order form on page 95.

BEAUTY FROM ASHES

Readings for times of loss

JENNIFER REES LARCOMBE

'When my life seemed burnt to ashes, the last thing I could cope with was reading lengthy Bible passages, yet the Bible contains many verses which encourage and comfort people who are grappling with grief and loss. I began collecting these verses and sticking them all over my kitchen walls! My favourite verse reminded me that God could transform the ashes of my life into something new and beautiful. This book grew out of my collection of "kitchen verses", combined with some of the practical tips and helpful ideas for those adjusting to loss of various kinds, given to me at the time by others who know how it feels from personal experience.'

This is a book for keeping by the bedside, for dipping into just for a few moments every day, offering help along the way for the hardest of times.

ISBN 1 84101 124 X   £6.99
Available from your local Christian bookshop or, in case of difficulty, using the order form on page 95.